Psychomachia
<u>or</u> "The Fight for Mansoul":
Making Moral Sense of
Neo-Republican Economics

by ROBERT E. KOHN

Professor Emeritus of Economics

Southern Illinois University, Edwardsville

Copyright © September 2011 Robert E. Kohn

All rights reserved.

ISBN-13: 978-1493772735

ISBN-10: 1493772732

Front and back cover design by Michelle Volansky

Cover image: *Discussing Dreams with Henry Rousseau* by Robert R. Malone, 1982.

Lithograph on paper, 27.5" by 39.5" (2/50)

Photograph of lithograph by Andy Wise.

Book Formatting: Mira Digital Publishing; Anne Schonhardt, Production Technician.

Table of Contents

Introduction		5
Chapter One:	Prudentius's Fifth-Century Christian Morality	11
Chapter Two	The Second Brain: *Stomacho*	19
Chapter Three:	Virtues, Vices, and the Old-Economics	23
Chapter Four:	Musgrave's Generalization of Keynes's *General Theory*	41
Chapter Five:	Faith-Based Neo-Economics	53
Chapter Six:	9/11 and the Re-recognition of Good Versus Evil	59
Chapter Seven:	Dystopia and Neo-Postmodernism	65
Chapter Eight:	Conclusion	77
Epilogue		81
Works Cited		86
Index		92

How often, when the plaguing sins
have been driven away,
have we felt our soul aglow
with the presence of God,
how often, after these pure joys,
felt our heavenly nature grow cool
and yield to foul desire!
Savage war rages hotly,
rages within our bones,
and man's two-sided nature is
in an uproar of rebellion;
for the flesh that was formed of clay
bears down upon the spirit,
but again the spirit that issued
from the pure breath of God
is hot within the dark
prison-house of the heart,
and even in its close bondage
rejects the body's filth.
Light and darkness
with their opposing spirits are at war,
and our two-fold being inspires powers
at variance with each other,
until Christ our God comes to our aid,
orders all the jewels of the virtues in a pure setting,
and where sin formerly reigned
builds the golden courts of his temple,
creating for the soul,
out of the trial of its conduct,
ornaments for rich Wisdom to find delight in
as she reigns for ever
on her beauteous throne.

H.J. Thomson's translation of lines 899-915 of Prudentius's P*sychomachia*, converted by the present author to free verse.

Psychomachia or "The Fight for Mansoul"

Introduction

I have begun writing this polemic on August 5, 2011, the day after the New York Stock Exchange plummeted 513 points, with more than 14 billion shares changing hands! The "waves of selling of stocks began in Europe and continued throughout the day in the United States" as "investors fled assets like stocks" and "piled into the perceived safety of United States Treasuries" (Graham Bowley A1, B6). The drop reflected in part the world's alarm—and probably the imminent downgrade by Standard & Poor—that payments on US Treasury obligations could be suspended at the mere whim of Congress. It also reflected the investment community's reaction to the deal forged by Republicans "to cut spending by at least $2.4 trillion over ten years, with a multibillion-dollar down payment later this year," completing "an about-face in the federal government's role from outsize spending in the immediate aftermath of the recession to outsize cuts going forward" (Binyamin Appelbaum and Catherine Rampell A1). The President's insistence on new tax revenues in the mix, allowing wealthy Americans to bear their fair share of the burden, was shoved aside. After winning this "nasty debt ceiling duel," which had left "the country a cat's whisker from default," House Republicans, secure in the "feeling they have scored fiscal victories," are moving "on to an even bigger challenge: persuading voters, state legislators and Democrats to alter the Constitution with a balanced budget amendment" (Jennifer Steinhauer *Republicans Fresh* A10).

The one-sided agreement reached on Monday, August 1, 2011 is an unquestionable triumph for Republicans, who had every intention of defaulting on maturing US bonds if they did not get their way. The original Boston Tea Party was countered by Britain's so-called "Coercive Acts" intended to punish the American colonies. It is ironic that their modern namesake, the driving force behind Neo-Republicanism, mandates coercive acts intended to punish *their own* countrymen, beginning with middle-class public servants, first at the federal level

Introduction

and then, by extension, at the state and city levels. Presumably these jobs in the public sector would be replaced by "more legitimate," privately created ones, in the new prosperity fostered by the salvation of the Bush tax cuts and time-honored tax loopholes. At least that was the faith, absent any supportive theory, of Neo-Republican economics.

Brian Knowlton reported, when President Obama insisted on imposing "a minimum tax rate on those who earn more than $1 million a year," that Republican lawmakers responded that such threats "amounted to 'class warfare'" (Knowlton A19). To put this "warfare" into an historical context, the present polemic draws on the fifth century classic, *Psychomachia*, i.e., *The Fight for Man's Soul*, by the Latin poet Prudentius, as translated by H.J. Thomson. This paean to early Christianity is relevant to contemporary American politics where, since the beginning of the 21st century, government and religion have intermixed in right-wing politics. Prudentius's respect for Jewish antiquity—see his comments on Aaron (Thomson 341) and King Solomon (335)—together with his resentment that Jews spurned Christ—see Thomson (145, 161)—resonate in evangelical Christianity today. Law professor Paul Horwitz began his op-ed piece in the August 6, 2011 *New York Times* by announcing that "Today, Gov. Rick Perry of Texas is scheduled to appear at Reliant Stadium in Houston for 'The Response,' an all-day event of Christian-centered prayer and fasting intended, as Mr. Perry explains on the event's Web site, to address the various crises that have 'besieged" America" (A17). Prudentius anticipated the present conjunction of Christianity and American politics—actually it began 25 years earlier, in 380, with the Edict of Thessalonica, which some historians argue made Christianity the state religion of the Roman Empire—in his Preface when he thanked "His Grace the Emperor" for advancing him "in his service and rais[ing] me up, attaching me closer to him and bidding me stand in the nearest rank" (Thomson 3-5). An Italian teacher of history, Luisa Bagiotti, informs me that Prudentius owed his official career to his ability as a lawyer and a governor, that he devoted himself to religion after he retired (see Epilogue).

When I read in Horwitz's piece that the participation of the governor in a politically-oriented religious convocation had been challenged in the Courts, I immediately agreed that this convocation violated the separation of Church and State vouchsafed by the Constitution. But I was deeply moved by Horwitz's argument that "Religion plays too important a part in many people's lives to be denied a role in the public square," that "elected officials, like other citizens" should be "free to have and express religious views," and that to deny that right would deter believers, agnostics and atheists from reaching

> any kind of consensus. It will only impoverish the conversation, depriving many citizens of the ability to make, and judge, arguments that reflect their most cherished views. [...] Some people think we would be better off without religion in public life. In the long run, however, we would lose much more than we have to gain. Our debates may be more contentious if we allow religion in, but they will also be more committed and honest. Just as the Constitution allows Mr. Perry to stake his political future on 'The Response,' so it allows the rest of us to answer back.
> (Horwitz A17)

When, to the contrary, "religion is viewed as a fundamentally private matter," Horwitz explained, "the natural corollary is to think that it is inappropriate to criticize someone's faith" (A17). If I have accomplished no more for myself in undertaking this polemic than to have learned this lesson from Horwitz, it will have been worth it.

As a consequence, I now feel comfortable in reinterpreting Prudentius's *Psychomachia* in the context of the modern world. I also feel more comfortable stating that I reject religious fundamentalism, whether it is Jewish Fundamentalism spurring ethnic cleansing in the West Bank (see Ilan Pappe), Muslim Fundamentalism plotting the deaths of civilians, or Christian

Introduction

Fundamentalism, of whose holy commandments and ethical doctrines, Fredric Jameson wrote that "casuistry has long since settled the matter; they [...] need no longer be taken literally" (390). When

> confronted with properly modern forms of injustice, bureaucratic warfare, systemic or economic inequality, and so forth, modern [evangelical] theologians and churchmen can work up persuasive accommodations to the constraints of complex modern societies, and provide excellent reasons for bombing civilian populations or executing criminals which do not disqualify the executors from Christian status. (Jameson 390)

Whether the American Family Association, the principal organization behind Governor Perry's "The Response" in Houston, is fundamentalist I cannot say, though Horwitz notes that their "vitriolic stance on issues like gay rights have led the Southern Poverty Law Center to call it a 'hate group'"—to his credit, "Mr. Perry has tried to distance himself from some of these views" (17A).

It is understandable that some people would hate homosexuality. The "whole field of evolutionary psychology," writes Joseph Carroll, is "devoted to (in this order): survival, sex and mating, parenting and kinship, and group living" (*Literary Darwinism* 107). Carroll's thesis that authors are motivated to write, and readers to prefer, literature that reflects their genetic drive to continue the species, would limit their literary interest in homosexuality. Whichever genes explain homosexuality, it is unlikely that they would have been selected for survival. Literary Darwinism is a powerful new hermeneutic but in some cases such as this, it does not reflect the recent reality of human overpopulation and its consequent threat to biodiversity and therefore to the survival of the human species as well (see Kohn, *Thresholds and Complementarities in an Economic Model of Preserving and Conserving Biodiversity*). One of the most functional families I personally know consists of two fathers and a son that one of them fathered via artificial insemination of a lesbian woman whom he knows professionally. That the son has excelled attests to the wholesomeness of his periodic rotation between two loving family environments, one with two fathers and the other with two mothers.

Though I may understand, without sympathizing, why some people would hate homosexuality, I cannot understand the hatred manifested in the following letter from a reader of the *St. Louis Post-Dispatch*, published yesterday, August 6, 2011. Entitled "Know-it-all," it read as follows:

> Every time Paul Krugman's column appears, I cringe. His suggestions in "Catastrophe was not averted" (Aug. 2) about further government spending are the kind of thinking that got us into the mess we're in, the recent "deal" notwithstanding. His hateful tone, his know-it-all orthodoxy, and the better-than-everyone-else attitude he freely attributes to his having won an ill-bestowed Nobel Prize all should cause the *Post-Democrat* to cancel its agreement with him. Give us columnists who can present a more nuanced view of things, who do not constantly whine about opposing viewpoints and who can engage in a dialogue on the merits of an issue without descending into childish diatribes. (A11)

As to Krugman's Nobel Prize, an economist friend of mine, David Pines of Tel-Aviv University, who was my chief post-doctoral mentor, once told me that his field, urban and regional economics, had been struggling to survive and might have gone under, if it had not been for Paul Krugman. By publishing a major article extending the latest theory of international trade to urban and regional economics, Krugman generated a renaissance in his field. Based on David's gratitude for that achievement, I have looked upon Krugman as the second most important American economist, second only to his teacher at M.I.T., Paul Samuelson.

I hope in this polemic, if not to make sense of Neo-Republican economics, to at least understand why its leading advocates would feel morally justified, which I presume they do, in taking the extreme economic positions they take. I will try to see them in the roles of Prudentius's high-principled Virtues

Introduction

battling against the wrong-headed Vices. The biggest challenge will be finding a Virtue to match House majority leader Eric Cantor, who insisted that any federal disaster aid for victims of Tropical Storm Irene must "be offset by an equal amount in spending cuts to keep the federal deficit from growing," even though fellow Neo-Republicans pleaded "that helping people whose lives have been upended by the storm should take precedent over managing the budget deficit" and "strongly disagreed with the notion of delaying aid to find cuts elsewhere in the budget" (Raymond Hernandez A24). Although I am writing this polemic in chronological order, the reader may note that I insert later newspaper reports as I reread what I have written—this is almost a diary, but not quite.

What it is is the struggle of an 83 year old ex-utopian, on the border of senility, to come to terms aesthetically as well as rationally with a world turned dystopian, but still wondrous. A polyglot of economics, literary criticism, ancient history and newspaper articles, it is a quirky, over-the-top venture into extreme interdisciplinarity and intertextuality. What it lacks in focus and synthesis, it hopefully makes up in synergies and original ideas. As a token of my apology, I shall price the book as low as I possibly can and still cover the short-run variable costs of printing and vending.

Psychomachia or "The Fight for Mansoul"

Chapter One

Prudentius's Fifth-Century Christian Morality

I learned about Prudentius in 2004 or 2005 when I read Brian McHale's reference in *Postmodernist Fiction* to "[v]ariations on the venerable mode of psychomachia," allegories which "typically involve the confrontation of warring principles, semantic oppositions personified" (142). So influential was Prudentius's confrontation of warring principles that it started a genre in medieval literature. Whereas the "ancient psychomachias characteristically pitted personified Good against personified Evil," McHale explained, what postmodernism posed as polar opposites turn out "to contain elements or traces of its opposed term" (142, 144). In effect, the "symmetries are systematically undone, the polar opposites allowed to 'bleed' into one another" (144). This happens not at all in Prudentius's *Psychomachia*—good is good and evil is evil, and never the twain shall commingle.

Aurelius Prudentius Clemens was born "in the year 348 [, …] most likely […] at Caesaraugusta (Saragossa)" in Roman Spain (Thomson vii). This was well before the time of Galileo, when people still believed that the sun circled the earth rather than the other way around. The year of Prudentius's death is not known, but he had already reached his 57th year when he began the preface to his book of poems as follows:

> Full fifty years, if I err not, have I lived, and beyond that it is the seventh time that the heaven is wheeling the year and I have the benefit of the circling sun. The end is close upon me, and by now what God is adding to my days is on the border of old age. (Thomson 3)

Asking forgiveness for the "sinful falsehoods" and "lewd sauciness and wanton indulgence" that "marred my youth" (3), Prudentius resolved,

> as my last end draws near [, to] let my sinning soul put off her folly [, and let] no night pass without singing of her Lord. Let her [Prudentius perceives his soul as feminine] fight against heresies, expound the

> Catholic faith, trample on the rites of the heathen, strike down thy Idols, O Rome, devote song to the martyrs, and praise the apostles. (Thomson 5)

Prudentius's *Psychomachia,* the best known of his works during the middle ages, was unique in its feminine personifications of the lightly armed Virtues, warriors for Jesus Christ, and the aggressively armed Vices, followers of Belial (Thomson 329), who in grisly single combats battled to the death. The "Fight for Mansoul" took on personal meaning for me in 2006, when the State of Missouri was locked in a bitter battle over a constitutional amendment—this was during the second Bush's presidency, and the amendment had been proposed to forestall pending Missouri restrictions on the use of embryonic stem cells—that would have allowed medical researchers and their patients to develop procedures in which these cells could be used to cure diabetes, Parkinson's disease, Alzheimer's, cancer and other serious maladies, without fear of threatened state penalties as severe as incarceration. I couldn't understand why so many conservative Christians were adamant that embryonic stem cells, no longer needed by their donors, had to be respectfully disposed of rather than used for anything, however beneficial, other than the reproductive purpose that God in their view had intended. But I could respect the sincerity of Prudentius's faith that "man's body lost its primeval nature" when

> power from on high created a new flesh, and a woman unwedded conceived the God Christ, who is man in virtue of his mortal mother but God along with the Father [, that f]rom that day all flesh is divine, since it conceives Him and takes on the nature of God by a covenant of partnership. For the Word made flesh has not ceased to be what it was before, that is the Word, by attaching to itself the experience of the flesh; its majesty is not lowered by the experience of the flesh, but raises men to nobler things. (Thomson 285)

Psychomachia or "The Fight for Mansoul"

In an endnote to my essay on Jacques Derrida, I recall my own childhood infatuation with "Mary, full of grace" (*A Derridean Look* n8, 405). With the help of James Rives, a prominent authority on Christianity's rise in the final centuries of the Roman Empire, I tried and failed to publish a paper respectfully contrasting the conservative Christian view I learned from Prudentius with my own view that if scientists can prove—and they should be free to try to—that embryonic stem cells can reduce human morbidity, that would take precedence over faith-based impedimenta, however sincere.

Now, five years later, in the heat of the so-called debt crisis, another battle turns me back to Prudentius's *Psychomachia*. Again there is a conflict in which faith and logic are in deep conflict. I hope to better understand the feelings of the self-righteous Neo-Republicans, who triumphed in the Congressional debt battle, by imagining them from the perspectives of Prudentius's triumphant heroines, one of whom was actually named "Righteousness" (Thomson 297). The sad letter to the editor of the *Post-Dispatch*, criticizing the hateful-toned Krugman, evokes some of the virtuous qualities that triumphed in fifth century *Psychomachia*. To match the ancient poet's gendering of his warriors, I will henceforth refer to both the letter writer and the hateful-toned economist as female combatants.

Every time Krugman's column appears, the letter-writer says, she anxiously cringes; and yet she bravely reads on. She is Prudentius's mild Virtue, ycleped "Long-Suffering," waiting "with staid countenance," while the economist is "swelling Wrath, showing her teeth with rage and foaming at the mouth" (Thomson 287). "Here's for thee," Wrath cries, "Receive the death stroke in thy calm breast, and betray no pain, since it is dishonor in thine eyes to utter a cry of pain" (287). So speaks Wrath, and her sharpened pine-shaft

> goes hissing after her angry words. Sure aimed, it hits the very stomach and smites hard with full force, but is struck off by the resistance of a hard cuirass, and rebounds; for the Virtue had prudently put on her shoulders a three-ply corselet of mail impenetrable. (289)

Wrath rages in ungoverned frenzy, spends her strength, then casts away the luckless arms that had been false to her. Beside herself in fury,

> wild passion fires her to slay herself. One of the many missiles that she had scattered without effect she picks up from the dust of the field. [...] fixes in the ground and with the upturned point stabs herself, piercing her breast with a burning wound. Standing over her, Long-Suffering cries:

"We have overcome a proud Vice with our wonted virtue." (291)

Appreciatively, I learn that Long-Suffering had been "escorted by a noble man," himself the famous

> Job had clung close to the side of his invincible mistress throughout the slaughter of many a foe, but now with a smile on his stern face as he thought of his healed sores and, by the number of his scars, recounted his thousands of hard-won fights, his own glory, and his foes' dishonor. (Thomson 291)

Clearly, this was the Job of the *Jewish Bible*, though Prudentius would have called it the *Old Testament* (Thomson 202n).

With Wrath's demise, the poet's attention turns to ireful Pride, "galloping about, all puffed up" (291), looking down "with swelling disdain" upon "the force that confronts her; a force small in number and scantily armed, that Lowliness had gathered for the war" (293). What chance has this motley crew against the ill-bestowed Nobel laureate, Pride herself, armored with know-it-all orthodoxy and imbued with her haughty better-than-anyone-else attitude? The slain Wrath transmogrified, Pride derides the assembled "spiritless, luckless, base, insensate foe," scorning their unwarlike spirit (225). "Is Chastity's cold stomach of any use in war, or Brotherly Love's soft work done by stress of battle? [...] I shall have this feeble band trodden down like stubble" (295, 297). Thanks to the inept interference of Deceit, another "of those cursed plagues, the Vices," Pride is unhorsed, but likewise the unpretentious princess Lowliness is almost trapped in the pit that Deceit has dug. But Hope, Lowliness's loyal comrade, comes to her aid, grasps threatening Pride by the hair,

> turns her face upwards; then, though she begs for mercy, bends the neck, severs the head, lifts it and holds it up by the dripping locks. Hope with her pure lips upbraids the dead Vice: "An end to thy big talk! God breaks down all arrogance. Greatness falls; the bubble bursts; swollen pride is flattened. [...] Well known and true is the saying of our Christ that the lowly ascend to high places and the proud are reduced to low degree. (299)

The bubble's burst would likely gratify the cringing letter-writer, who scorned Wrath's/Pride's appeal for government spending because it was the kind of thinking that got the country into the terrible mess we're in.

The letter-writer's stouthearted conviction that her forthright epistle will move the *Post-Dispatch* to cancel its agreement with Krugman evokes the virtuous Faith, who when she enters the field to face the doubtful chances of battle,

> takes no thought to gird on arms or armor, but trusting to a stout heart and unprotected limbs challenges the hazards of furious warfare, meaning to break them down. Lo, first Worship-of-the-Old-Gods [replacing fallen Wrath and Pride] ventures to match her strength against Faith's challenge and strike at her. (Prudentius 281)

That Governor Perry would lead an all-day event of Christian-centered prayer and fasting "to address the various crises that have 'besieged' America" suggests that Prudentius's fifth-century fight for man's soul has moved from the sacerdotal to the political-economic arena (Horwitz A17). Instead of Pagan goddesses like Diana, Minerva and Venus, the spurned sisters of the modern-day Vice, "Worship-of-the-Old-Gods," have disreputable names like Big-Government (Starve-the-Beast), Job-Killing-Regulation, Federal-Debt, Distributional-Equity, Public-Good, Double-Tax, Inheritance-Tax, Climate-Science, Entitlement, Stimulus, Obamacare and Labor-Unions. Prudentius lumped the likes of them together in the shifty "Indulgence," who "had long lost her repute" (Thomson 301). Opposed to the foe Indulgence are modern Virtues such as Balanced-Budget, No-New-Revenue and Jobs-Jobs-Jobs, while Vices such as Inheritance-Tax, Counseling-for-End-of-Life and Public-Sector are recognized for what they really are: Death-Tax, Death-Panel, and Big-Government-on-My-Back. The "maiden Chastity" (283), Faith's first mentioned ally "on the grassy field" of battle is the adored Virtue that courageously opposes such Vices as Sex-Education-in-Public-Schools and Gay-Marriage, modern names for all the Vices that Prudentius lumped under "Lust" (283).

When Worship-of-the-Old-Gods ventures to match her strength against Faith's challenge, the latter "rising higher, smites her foe's head down, with its fillet-decked brows, lays in the dust that mouth that was sated with the blood of beasts, and tramples the eyes under foot, squeezing them out in death" (Thomson 281). It is even more bloody when the "maiden Chastity" is attacked by "Lust the Sodomite"; the former "undismayed smites" back, and "with a sword-thrust she pierces the disarmed harlot's throat," the latter spewing "out hot fumes with clots of foul blood" (283). This was written early in Christian history, and the influence of the Jewish Bible and Roman paganism is much in evidence. Prudentius follows the death of Lust the Sodomite with references to the "severed head of Holofernes," which had "soaked his Assyrian chamber with his lustful blood, and the unbending Judith, spurning the lecherous captain's jeweled couch" from the *Book of Judith* in the Hebrew *Apocrypha* (Thomson 283). When he wrote these bloody passages, Prudentius may have had in mind the *taurobolium*, the pagan initiation that Bertrand Lançon reported Prudentius had seen and described as "an idolatrous and disgusting rite" in which the aspiring novice lay "[s]tretched out beneath a hurdle on which a bull had its throat cut," causing him or her to be "drenched in its blood as the pledge of a new life" (Lançon 91). With respect to bloody battles one-on-one and the involvement of women, Prudentius is likewise recorded by Lançon as having witnessed some of the "last gladiatorial combats" in the Empire, and registering abhorrence at "the cruel pleasure derived from these gory fights by the Vestal Virgins," who would rise "from their seats as the decisive blows were struck," and gesture "with their thumbs in order to see the losers finished off" (144). Rives tell us that "'paganism' did not die of natural causes, but was deliberately murdered" (23). Prudentius appears to have contributed to that "murder." "In the Graeco-Roman tradition, diversity of cult practice was, like the multiplicity of [pagan] divinities, taken as the norm" (Rives 24). And "if diversity of practice was regarded as the norm, diversity of belief was hardly even noticed" (25). The Christian concern for "[h]omogeneity of religious practice and belief, then, was almost completely alien to the Graeco-Roman religious tradition" (25). It fits this pattern that the Neo-Republicans share a relatively homogeneous philosophy, differing less in policies than in how far they should be taken, whereas Democrats attack each other on such basic issues as free trade, labor unionization, foreign wars, and so forth.

Finally, back to the task of matching Eric Cantor with his Virtue. He understands that Neo-Republican representatives from storm-ravaged states are anxious to have "all the resources necessary to recover from Hurricane Irene" and doesn't want to "let politics get in the way of doing the right thing for our families and communities that have been affected by the desire," but he equates the government's position to that of a family that has maxed out on its credit card and needs to sacrifice: "it finds the money to take care of a sick loved one or what have you, and then goes without trying to buy a new car or an addition onto the house" (Hernandez A25). Cantor's Virtue could be "poverty-stricken Honesty, dried-up Soberness [...], Purity with scarce a tinge of blood to color her cheeks" or given his willingness to do without, "white-faced Fasting" (Thomson 297).

Psychomachia or "The Fight for Mansoul"

Chapter Two

The Second Brain: *Stomacho*

Sadly for the medieval Christian readers of Prudentius's triumphant Virtues, the glow of victory they engendered was short-lived. The fighting was more important than the winning:

> How often, when the plaguing sins have been driven away, have we felt our soul aglow with the presence of God, how often, after these pure joys, felt our heavenly nature grow cool and yield to foul desire! Savage war rages hotly, rages within our bones, and man's two-sided nature is in an uproar of rebellion. (343).

Like Prudentius, his early devotees must also have had hearts that were at bottom "foul with the filth of sin" (Thomson 341), leading them to painful self-incrimination, which in turn "yields to foul desire!" (343). But what exactly is *foul* desire, and how does it relate to *"stomacho!"* in the accompanying Latin text, the corresponding lines of which are

> *o quotiens animam, vitiorum peste repulsa,*
> *sensimus incaluisse Deo! quotiens tepefactum*
> *caeleste ingenium post gaudia candida taetro*
> *cessisse stomacho! Fervent bella horrida, fervent*
> *ossibus inclusa, fremit et discordibus armis*
> *non simplex natura hominis.* (Lines 899-904, Thomson 342)

Remembering very little of my high-school Latin, I was fortunate in being able to access the above-cited classics scholar, James Rives, and request a more current translation of the above Latin excerpt from *Psychomachia*. Rives, the Kenan Eminent Professor of Classics at the University of North Carolina at Chapel Hill, had been my son Daniel's roommate at Washington University. In an email dated September 25, 2006, he obliged me with the following:

Oh, how often have we perceived that our soul, once the plague of sins has been driven away, has grown hot for God! How often [have we perceived that] our heavenly nature, grown lukewarm after pure joys, has yielded to black anger [or desire]! Savage wars seethe, they seethe enclosed in our bones, and the un-simple nature of man roars with discordant arms.

Along with his translation, James explained that

"*stomachus*" means literally "stomach," perceived as the source of appetites and often used metaphorically to mean "anger, irritation." "*Simplex*" means "having only one layer" or "having only one constituent element," hence Thomson translates "non simplex" as "two-sided." So there are few things one could quibble with, but in general I don't see a way to significantly improve what Thomson does. I'm sorry that I can't be more helpful; let me know if you have more questions.   Yours, James

Appropriately, it seems, James substitutes "black anger," connoting belligerence, for Thomson's "foul desire," which is ambiguous in the context of Prudentius's poem. It is "savage war," either within-people or between-people or both, that Prudentius's text explicitly vociferates. President Obama, seemingly forced to capitulate after the Democrat-controlled Senate finessed the promised fight, "rolled over and rolled over," a Minnesotan Democrat complained, to avoid a fight; whereas, to the contrary, Representative Tom Graves, black with anger, had preferred to default on Treasury oligations if the Neo-Republicans did not get their way. When he told his town hall audience that he didn't "believe [in] compromises," he "was met with "thunderous applause" (Steinhauer *Fight Harder* A13).

Rives's focus on the stomach as the center of anger and irritation was timely. Dr. Michael Gershon had recently accrued national acclaim for his book on the stomach, entitled *The Second Brain: The Scientific Basis of Gut Instinct and a Groundbreaking New Understanding of Nervous Disorders of the Stomach and Intestine.*

Psychomachia or "The Fight for Mansoul"

Frustration and anger in the brain can certainly make the stomach "churn away in high dudgeon," and the "link of gastric acidity to anxiety" had understandably and long "led people to believe that ulcer disease was a psychosomatic illness" (105). Gershon was one of the early researchers that suspected that "anxiety might be a *consequence*, rather than a *cause*, of the majority of ulcers" (107). By the mid-1980s, it was confirmed that

> Ulcers are a symptom of an infectious disease caused by *Heliocobacter pylori*, a peculiar organism that manages to avoid getting killed by the stomach's hydrochloric acid. [... Fortunately, t]he antibiotic, Biaxin (clarithromycin), for example, wipes out Heliocobacter over 90 percent of the time when it is combined with Prilosec (omeprazole). (Gershon 108)

It is not surprising that the fifth-century Romans believed that the stomach was the source of anger and irritation. It still is, though to a much lesser extent with the new drugs, because a still-significant source of emotional distress originates, not in the brain with anxiety, but in the stomach from locally-caused pains there. That the stomach itself can be thought of as a brain was justified by the discovery that when "the vagus nerves are cut, a patient's brain and his/her stomach" are "completely independent of one another. [... T]he enteric nervous system perseveres after the brain is cut off" (Gershon 109). Prudentius did a service by providing a model of behavior in which human actions are based not only on thoughts and emotions originating in the brain, but also on gut responses to pains in the stomach and intestinal system. Just as the early Christians responded to those gut feelings, so do the Neo-Republicans today. From time to time, my gut powers dominate my thoughts, and I do and say things that I usually regret. Prudentius has helped me to understand this aspect of myself, and understanding is power.

Psychomachia or "The Fight for Mansoul"

Chapter Three
Virtues, Vices and the Old-Economics

In the Neo-Republican economic version of the fight for man's soul, such original Virtues that Prudentius called Faith, Long-Suffering, Lowliness, Righteousness, Soberness, Thrifty, Good Works and Concord, now include Balanced-Budget, No-New-Revenue and Jobs-Jobs-Jobs. Vices that bore names like Worship-of-the-Old-Gods, Wrath, Lust, Pride, Deceit, Indulgence, Desire, Ostentation, Greed, Corruption, Treachery, Falsehood, Crime, Love-of-Possession, Avarice, Violence, Fraud and Discord are now joined by Socialism, Death-Tax, Death-Panel, Double-Tax, Big-Government, Job-Killing-Regulation, Deficit, Debt, Entitlement, Distributional-Equity, Public-Handout, Climate-Science, Stimulus, Obamacare and Labor-Union. In the present context, Worship-of-the-Old-Gods is now Worship-of-the-Old-Economics.

I still have the public finance textbook, *The Theory of Public Finance* by Richard Musgrave, that I used when I returned to college in 1966 for my master's and doctoral degrees. When I retrieved and started to read it, I realized that the economic principles I live by are rooted in its pages. Here were the Old-Economics that the Neo-Republican Virtues want to lay in the dust, that the *Post-Dispatch* letter-writer believed had "got us into the mess we're in." It fits in with the Vices of *Psychomachia* that the title of that letter-to-the-editor, "Know-It-All," which referred to Paul Krugman, was similarly hyphenated. This text inaugurated what became known as "Modern Public Finance" and dated back for its conception to Musgrave's own "doctoral dissertation, where [he said he] first attempted to come to grips with what may be called an economic theory of budget determination" (v). What could be more relevant to this polemic than that?

"Most of the early discussion of fiscal policy," wrote Musgrave, "was developed against the background of the stagnation hypothesis" (498). The three parameters of his public finance model were then, as they should be now, **t**, the average rate of tax on **Y**, a country's total income (434), and **g**, the "fraction of product [also **Y**] bought by government" (367n). Assuming that **g** is fixed by what Musgrave idealistically called "the Allocation Branch" of the government, it follows that

> The value of **t** must then be adjusted to assure the equilibrium rate of growth. If this leaves us with **t** = **g**, equilibrium growth at the given level of **g** requires a balanced budget, If it leaves us with **t** < **g**, it requires a constant rate of deficit […] If it leaves us with **t** > **g**, a constant rate of surplus is called for. One may wish to refer to a situation where **t** < **g** as one of stagnation. (Musgrave 499)

The United States National Income, **Y**, reported in the *Statistical Abstract of the United States: 2011*, U.S. Census Bureau, is 12.288 trillion dollars for the latest reported year, 2009. (Table 672, page 440). Correcting for inflation and allowing for the anemic growth of **Y** the next year, I will round out the 2009 figure to 13 trillion dollars for 2010, the year for which the remaining statistics are given. Estimated US Government Receipts in 2010 were 2.2 trillion dollars and Government Outlays were 3.7 trillion dollars (Table 467, page 310). It follows that **t** = (2.2)/(13) = 0.17, that **g** = (3.7)/(13) = 0.28 and that the Gross Federal Deficit according to the Musgrave model was (**t** - **g**)(13) = 1.4 trillion dollars. This corresponds to the Government's own estimate of the deficit—total receipts minus total outlays—for 2010, which was 1.929 trillion dollars minus 3.315 trillion, equal to a deficit in 2010 of approximately 1.4 trillion dollars (Table 467, page 310).

Neo-Republicans insisted, and were willing to default on the Treasury's obligations unless their demand was met, on a 1.5 trillion dollar reduction of the total debt by reducing **g** alone rather than by a combination of increasing **t** and reducing **g**. In effect, they repudiated in its entirety what Musgrave in his Preface called a

> general framework for an economic theory of the public household, combining the functional finance of the stabilization type with other equally important objectives of budget policy, including provision for the satisfaction of social wants and adjustments in the distribution of income. (vii)

Musgrave went on to

> beg the reader not to discard this somewhat utopian scheme with the sterile objection of 'utterly impracticable.' Let its practicability be tested not by prospects for speedy enactment but by the contribution it has to make to orderly thinking about the basic issues of budget policy. (vii)

I had not read Musgrave's *Preface* for forty years, if at all, and was surprised to see his reference to utopia, because it was not until 2009 that I discovered and reported the following in a brief bio accompanying an article in the *Journal of Modern Jewish Studies* that began as follows:

> Robert E. Kohn: Professor Emeritus of Economics at Southern Illinois University, Edwardsville, was, until well after his retirement, an unwitting utopian economist, unaware that his modernist faith in perfectly competitive markets and the government's commitment to fostering distributional equity had been repudiated by more savvy postmodern economists. (317)

I should note that the unwitting witness that I wrote about in this article was not myself but a beloved New York rabbi who repudiated his long-held modernist utopian expectations in a sermon in 1975, a third of a century before I recognized my expectations for what they were. That my economic thinking from beginning to end remained utopian explains a fundamental bias on my part against the dystopian, from-the-gut, economics of the Neo-Republicans.

It was during the 1950s, the peak of utopian modernism, that Musgrave wrote his textbook. It must have been he who started me off on that bent, though the professor who taught the course stamped it in. It says something important that that professor was Murray Wiedenbaum, who eventually became President Nixon's Assistant Secretary of the Treasury for Economic Policy and subsequently President Reagan's first chairman of his Council of Economic Advisers. That my first teacher became a conservative Republican and I a liberal Democrat attests to the empirical, logical foundation on which economic theory rests, or at least did when I was part of it. Unlike the Neo-Republicans today, Murray is a classical Republican, who, in Tony Judt's words, has "a well-grounded distaste for over-hasty change," which happily accords with my belief in incremental fine-tuning (3). The essence of Musgrave's general framework for an economic theory of the public household is its division of government fiscal responsibilities into three idealized divisions: the Allocation, Distribution, and Stabilization Branches. The Allocation Branch is dedicated to securing an efficient allocation of the nation's resources between the private sector and the public sector, which includes regulating the former in the public interest and ordaining an optimal mix of public goods, such as roads and government facilities, and public services, such as legal adjudication, defense, and social insurance. The Distribution Branch determines "what steps are needed to establish the desired or 'proper' state of distribution" of both income and wealth, such steps including progressive tax systems and inheritance taxes (Musgrave 5). Finally, the Stabilization Branch decides "what must be done to secure price-level stability and full employment" (5).

Musgrave said something important about his public finance model when he simplified matters by assuming that the value of **g** is "fixed by the Allocation Branch. The value of **t** must then be adjusted to assure the equilibrium rate of growth [of **Y**]" (499). That **g** is fixed by the Allocation Branch, implies that, for the targeted rate of economic growth and the corresponding value of **Y** estimated by the Stabilization Branch, there is an optimal value of **g** that should be accepted as a datum by the other two branches. I like to think that **g** is the weighted average of individual components, g_1, g_2, g_3, etc., each one corresponding to an optimal level or quantity of some different public good or service. It is optimal in the sense that the marginal social benefit of each budgeted level equals the marginal social cost of providing it. The major follow-up that Wiedenbaum brought to the course, on which we then spent much of our time, was the implementation of individual benefit/cost analyses. For my own I calculated the ratio of total benefits to total costs, i.e., **B/C**, of a program that would ban the burning of leaves in the City of Clayton, MO, where I then lived and still do. It turned out fortuitously that the U.S. Public Health Service, the precursor of the U.S. Environmental Protection Agency, was interested in the possibility of air pollution control by recycling leaves instead of burning them, and because my study, which I was able to publish in a scholarly magazine, was the first of its kind and the results were favorable, they ordered 20,000 reprints of my article for disseminating to state and local government agencies.

It was interesting that all of my benefit/cost analyses argued for the expansion of the public sector, whereas Wiedenbaum enhanced his reputation as a conservative economist by identifying public goods and services that should be contracted or eliminated because their benefit/cost ratios were less than unity. Assuming, which Musgrave might have done implicitly (There is no entry for Benefit/Cost or Cost/Benefit Analysis in his Index), that all public outlays were subject to fine-tuning, informed by this opposition of positively and negatively biased analysts, one could believe that the corresponding level of government outlays, **gY**, was optimal, and that the tax schedule should be adjusted so that total government receipts, **tY**, would generate either the desired deficit—when, according to the Stabilization Branch, **Y** needed stimulation expenditures—or else the desired surplus when excess demand was anticipated and past debt should be retired. In the special case of a perfect allocation in which **t** = **g** and resources are fully employed, marginal benefits of public goods and services would in theory equal their respective marginal costs, while the prices of privately produced goods and services would equal their respective marginal costs. It was an elegant model, and it underlay almost every one of the 99 papers I published when I was an economist. Of course, there is no such a thing as a perfect allocation; it is predicated on perfectly competitive markets and on what Samuelson called "omniscient" government planners. It is a utopian dream. But I believe that it's closer to being right than the dystopian nightmare that the Neo-Republicans would have us embrace. It is not as though they believe that public goods and services have been carried to extremes in which marginal costs exceed marginal benefits, or that, however worthwhile they may be, the country cannot afford to pay for them. It is rather that public goods and services are intrinsically insidious, productive of sloth and dependency, and worst of all, emblematic of the insidious Vice, socialism. In the lead editorial in the August 25, 2011 issue of *The New York Times*, the Editors alleged that Governor Perry of Texas said that "he wants to make [national] government 'inconsequential'" (A22). In terms of the fight for man's soul, Perry surely sees himself as one of the godly Virtues, destined to conquer the slothful Vices.

Neo-Republican economics began with President Reagan's denunciation of Big Government—not at all a solution to national problems, he said, but the problem itself. In all fairness to Reagan, he could have been reacting to the deluge of earmarks for local "pork" projects that Congress was forcing him to sign into law. If those projects had survived the careful benefit/cost criteria that Wiedenbaum so strongly advocated, they would not have been dismissed as "pork." I don't know that Reagan was thusly motivated, but it is helpful for understanding his apparently genuine moral concern at the time. Even Perry's disdain for public sector spending may have a reasonable explanation; according to the above mentioned editorial in *The New York Times*, many of the "nearly 600 boards, commissions, authorities and departments in Texas […] are of little use to the public and should have long been shut down or consolidated" (A22). Instead, they "are of great use to the governor, who more than any predecessor has created thousands of potential appointments for beneficent backers" (A22). Perry must think that he is doing nothing different than presidents do and have always done at the national level, though it also has to be his view that it is far less excusable there than at the State level.

Just as Neo-Republicans battle virtuously for an "inconsequential" level of domestic federal spending, they advocate for a low tax burden on citizens, and in the case of the Budget Control Act of 2011, they insisted successfully on no tax rate increases, not even the elimination of wasteful loopholes in the tax code. Representative Paul D. Ryan recently proclaimed that such tax increases would add "further instability to our system, more uncertainty, and it punished job creation" (Knowlton A19). The Neo-Republicans say that over and over again until people begin to believe it. The change they favor is to a flat, or at least flatter, range of tax rates that would allow lower income earners to share in the pride of paying their way too. Alternatively, Musgrave, taking his cue from John Stuart Mill (1806-1873), advocated higher tax rates on larger incomes "so as to minimize the total sacrifice involved," which would be "achieved by equating the marginal sacrifices of all taxpayers" (Musgrave 90). Take two households equal in every respect, number of children, medical needs, and so forth, except that one has an annual income of $50,000 and the other $100,000. Given a flat tax of 10 percent, the first household would pay $5,000 and the second would pay "10,000 per year. Assuming, as economists do, that we spend our money first on the things we need most, then on those we need less, and finally reach a point where we save in order to insure ourselves against possible declines in future income, it is reasonable to assume that if the first household, with net disposable income of $45,000, saves $1,000 for the future, the second household, whose net disposable income is $90,000, would more likely want to save, not $2,000 but, say $10,000. Obviously, the value of the first dollar of disposable income after taxes for the first household is greater than the corresponding value for the second household. To equate marginal sacrifice requires a higher than 10 percent tax on the larger income. This is the essence of what Musgrave calls "vertical equity" (160). It is conceivable that the heads of the lower income household grew up in extreme poverty and now think of themselves as very-well-to-do and happily save more than the higher income household saves, because the latter's heads were raised, say in mansions and find themselves financially strapped at the higher income. Such background considerations are ruled out by the Stabilization Branch, which treats all people as equal with respect to heritage.

The Neo-Republicans are disinclined to tax on the basis of equal marginal sacrifice because they believe that the more a person earns, the harder he or she will work (which is reasonable) and, as heads of businesses, the more he or she will be motivated to grow that business and employ additional people. However, the latter is not reasonable. A new worker (or new machine) is employed by a competitive firm when the marginal revenue that he or she or it will make possible for the firm exceeds its marginal cost, which, in the case of an employee, is the wage or salary he or she will be paid plus the payroll tax. Total profit is a residual, and allowing a firm to retain more of its profit or the hiring manager to pay a lower tax on his or her own income has no direct effect on the marginal revenue product of the potential employee and minimal effect on the demand for that firm's output. The mantra of the Neo-Republicans is "Jobs-Jobs-Jobs," and "Smaller-Government," which are incompatible. For a given state of technology, the only way to create jobs is to create new demand (raising the marginal revenue product of labor) or reducing the marginal cost of labor (the wage itself or the payroll tax). The President's effort to maintain the temporary reduction of workers' contributions to Social Security from 6.2 percent to 4.2 percent for another year is being contested by Neo-Republicans who argue "that such a cut adds needlessly to the nation's budget deficit, and should be replaced with an overhaul of tax policy instead" (Steinhauer *For Some in G.O.P.* A18). The President's decrease in the workers' portion of payroll taxes is not a saving for employers but an increase in employee disposable income and hence an increase in the general demand for goods, which raises the marginal revenue product of labor. Steinhauer reports that the Obama "administration is also mulling a similar tax cut for employers," which would act favorably and probably more effectively on the demand for labor (*For Some in G.O.P.* A18). It is not only the Neo-Republicans who have conflicting policies on labor; in an Op-Ed piece in the August 23, 2011 issue of *New York Times*, Joe Nocera criticized the National Labor Relations Board, most of whose top-level executives were appointed by Obama, for ordering Boeing Corporation to stop assembling the 787 Dreamliner airplane in its new 750-million dollar South Carolina plant in response to the Seattle union's complaint that the company opened the new facility

> to retaliate against the union, which has a history of striking at contract time. The N.L.R.B. solution, believe it or not, is to move all the Dreamliner production back to Puget Sound, leaving those 5,000 workers in South Carolina twiddling their thumbs. Seriously, when has a government agency ever tried to dictate where a company makes its products? (A21).

"As for the Republicans," Nocera concluded in the interest of fairness, "there are plenty of regulations that would actually help create jobs—but which they won't pass because of their own ideological blinders" (A21). In the interest of transparency, it behooves me to acknowledge, first, that most of the success I had in my first career as vice-president of a company that manufactured low-priced children's shoes in southern Missouri owed to the competitive advantage of low-cost, non-union labor in that region over that of the older establishments in New England, and second, that I own 224 shares of Boeing Company.

When Eric Cantor, the House majority leader, argued for an overhaul of tax policy, he had in mind the move toward a flat tax that would motivate the wealthy to "grow the economy and create jobs" (Steinhauer *For Some in G.O.P.* (A18). To my knowledge, Neo-Republicans have provided no empirical evidence to support their claim that higher marginal tax rates deter job creation on the part of high-earners. Above I invoke the standard, neoclassical economic argument that the demand for factors of production is independent of the tax that entrepreneur's pay on their personal income or their firm's total profit. In fact, I can give a counter example in which higher marginal tax rates on income lead to economic *expansion* and job *creation*. This example is from my own personal experience in the small shoe manufacturing company in which I held a minority interest, and my role was to design the shoes and to sell most of the output. The company and my income, which came entirely from commissions on my sales, grew steadily, and by the latter half of the 1950s I was in the top marginal tax bracket, 72-percent, earning over a hundred-thousand dollars a year. It was reassuring for me to sell more and more each year, and it became more important to maintain these increases, for my sake and the company's, than the extra, heavily taxed increments of annual income. I knew that our commission rate, 5-percent on sales, was high, having been established when we were making only baby shoes, a specialty item packaged in see-through plastic gift boxes. I sensed that competition was stiffening and that if the commission rate were cut to 3-percent, it would free a little over three cents per pair for niceties that our buyers liked. Chains and wholesalers paid $ 1.60 per pair for our children's shoes, which sold for $2.99 in ordinary retail establishments or Two-For-Five in the exploding self-service market. Three-cents went a long way when you were producing 5,000 pair a day. Inking the edges of the leather soles on girls' patent leather shoes may have cost a penny a pair in those days, but it made for a palpable improvement. My boss, who was my uncle, went along with lowering the commission rate. (Only recently have I learned from his daughter that he may have had some misgivings because he wanted me to accumulate enough money to buy out his majority share someday.)

  I was right that the shoes became easier to sell, which was important. I wasn't a particularly good salesman, and I wanted to be able to pressure my customers in a nice way by explaining that ours was a special deal—to get the attractive $1.60 price, buyers had to give me a signed order so we could start "cutting" the shoes at once. Yes, the high marginal tax rate motivated me to reduce the stress of my job, limit my travelling to three months for the spring line and another three months for the fall line, leaving three-month intervals between for styling. The increase in sales more than offset the cut in the commission rate, the firm grew to the point that people were driving as far as 50 miles to work in our factory. They worked on piece-rates, made much more than the minimum wage, and because we sold the factory out well in advance, could count on steady work and, when reorders started rolling in, on plenty of overtime.

My own example does not disprove the Neo-Republican contention that high tax rates on entrepreneurial compensation generally cause unemployment; surely they can come up with anecdotal examples counter to my own. But if they are to "overhaul tax policy" on that basis, they need to come up with compelling statistical evidence. It is unlikely that they can, given new information reported by David Kocieniewski that

> Recent history offers little evidence to support the contention that higher taxes undermine economic growth: employment and economic growth were far weaker after the Bush tax cuts of 2001 and 2004 than they were under the higher rates of the Clinton administration. (*A Tax Others Embrace* B2)

Neo-Republicans should also be mindful that the principles they are overhauling were formulated 150-years ago and fine-tuned from then on. Early Neo-Republicans have already done great harm in clobbering the principle of horizontal equity in taxation, according to which "an equal sacrifice should be imposed on people in equal positions" (Musgrave 160n). Under a recent Republican president, the tax laws were changed to eliminate dividends from the taxable income of recipients to the extent that the issuing corporation had already paid taxes on its income. Their argument was that taxing dividends was a double-tax on the income because the corporation had already paid the tax. One of the main advantages of owning shares in a corporation is that the corporation is considered a person in itself, which means that if the corporation goes bankrupt because it cannot pay its current liabilities, the creditors cannot collect what the corporation owes them from the share-holders who own or owned the corporation. Five years ago I bought some stock in a company that owned natural gas pipelines connecting producers with wholesale buyers. Shortly thereafter I received a prospectus from the company detailing its risks, one of which was stock-holder liability for environmental damage judgments against the company. I sold my stock as quickly as I could. Double-taxation is not the Vice that Neo-Republicans claim.

I didn't understand what Musgrave meant when he wrote that the "requirements of horizontal and vertical equity are but different sides of the same coin" (160), until I read the Op-Ed piece by Warren Buffett in the August 15, 2011 issue of *The New York Times*, in which he wrote that

> Last year my federal tax bill—the income tax I paid, as well as payroll taxes paid by me and on my behalf—was $6,938,744. That sounds like a lot of money. But what I paid was only 17.4 percent of my taxable income—and that's actually a lower percentage than was paid by any of the other 20 people in our office. Their tax burdens ranged from 33 percent to 41 percent and averaged 36 percent. (A19)

Presumably, a large part of Buffett's income were dividends on which, to avoid the phantom of double taxation, he paid little or no income tax. In that case, horizontal and vertical inequity are indeed the consequence of the same fault in the tax code.

The "average middle class family" in the United States, wrote Drew Westen, "has seen its income stagnate over the last 30 years while the richest 1 percent has seen its income rise astronomically" (7). Sabrina Tavernise reports that "More than one in three young families with children were living in poverty last year [. ...] At 37 percent, it was the highest level on record for the group" (*Poor Young* A19). The 400 richest people "control more of the wealth than 150 million of their fellow Americans" (Westen 7). In *Ill Fares the Land*, Tony Judt narrows in on the Wal-Mart founder's family, whose wealth "was estimated at about the same ($90 billion) as that of the bottom 40 percent of the US population: 120 million people" (14). Judt's book—the title of which is drawn from the lines "Ill fares the land, to hastening ills a prey/Where wealth accumulates and men decay" of Oliver Goldsmith's 1770 poem, *The Deserted Village*—attributes some of the worse ills in the United States to income inequality, which "is not just unattractive in itself; it clearly corresponds to pathological social problems that we cannot hope to address unless we attend to their underlying cause" (18). These include

> infant mortality, life expectancy, criminality, the prison population, mental illness, unemployment, obesity, malnutrition, teenage pregnancy, illegal drug use, economic insecurity, personal indebtedness and anxiety. [...] The wider the spread between the wealthy few and the impoverished many, the worse the social problems [. ...] Thus Sweden, or Finland, two of the world's wealthiest countries by per capita income or GDP, have a very narrow gap separating their richest from their poorest citizens—and they consistently lead the world in indices of measurable wellbeing. Conversely, the United States, despite its huge aggregate wealth, always comes low on such measures. We spend vast sums on healthcare, but life expectancy in the US remains below Bosnia and just above Albania. (16, 18).

Judt dates the extreme materialistic and selfish quality of contemporary American life "from the 1980s" (2). His dating of the turn accords with John Harwood's report on the "shift in inequality [...] when it came to the richest Americans. The top 1 percent (average 2007 income: $1.3 million) reaped 19.4 percent of the nation's total—double their 1979 share and more than the bottom 40 percent combined" (A17). Indeed, I remember the microeconomics textbook from the late 1970s that I taught from at Southern Illinois University Edwardsville, which proclaimed that poverty had been virtually eradicated. Less than 10 percent of American households were then below the poverty line and a relatively small total amount of annual transfer payments from the Federal government could bring them up to the official level of well-being. I am ashamed that I told my students—perhaps to show-off my presumed analytic skill, which makes it all the worse—that, of course, if we did give such transfer payments it would encourage poor people at or near the minimum level to work less than before and qualify for larger transfer payments, so that, in effect, the number earning below the poverty line would rise rather than fall further. Judt rebukes that kind of thinking as "economism," in this case, that poverty "is a natural condition of life about which we can do little," which is partly to blame for the "thirty years of growing *inequality*" that we have witnessed (Judt 21, 22). Musgrave may have anticipated that unfortunate growth when he let slip—back in 1959, the middle of the utopian Eisenhower years—his concern over the Government's "unwillingness to enforce even the degree of progression that has been provided for in the nominal structure of income tax rates" (167).

The "Personal Responsibility and Work Opportunity Act," signed by President Clinton in 1996 may have been part of the problem, though at the time I thought it was wise of the President to co-opt, closer to his own terms, an issue that Republicans were using against him. The purpose of the Act, as Judt explained it,

> was to shrink the nation's welfare rolls. This was to be achieved by withholding welfare from anyone who had failed to seek (and, if successful, accept) paid employment. Because an employer could thus hope to attract workers at almost any wage he offered—they could not decline a job, however distasteful, without risking exclusion from welfare benefits—not only were the numbers on welfare considerably reduced but wages and business costs fell too. (24)

I have no facts on the matter, but I suspect that Judt has overstated the case. Surely, an applicant could decline a job that would be distasteful and continue to search until she finds, at best, a job she really likes, at worst, the least distasteful job. Judt made it sound like the desperation of the applicants enabled the employers to impose a wage below the market equilibrium wage. This is unlikely. What happens whenever the supply of labor increases in a competitive labor market is that the equilibrium wage declines. Hopefully, there was some kind of government subsidy for employers who participated in Clinton's Work Opportunity Act.

Surely Judt was correct that welfare had "acquired an explicit stigma" (24), which is unfortunate. The Government had, for largely incorrect reasons, fostered increased inequality and failed to stimulate demand for labor that would have raised the market wage and attracted needy workers. Judt is right to scold us for having spoken "disparagingly of 'welfare queens'" (25). I never used the term but I presumed that it referred to women who "milked the system" in some underhanded way. Even if they did, what am I to think after I read Eric Lichtblau's article in *The New York Times* about "Representative Darrell Issa, the powerful Republican congressman" from California "Helping His District, and Himself" (A1). Among Lichtblau's allegations, which take up a third of the top-half of the front page and the entirety of page A13, is that Issa

> has secured millions of dollars in Congressional earmarks for road work and public works projects that promise improved traffic and other benefits to the many commercial properties he owns here north of San Diego. In one case, more than $800,000 in earmarks he arranged will help widen a busy thoroughfare in front of a medical plaza he bought for $10.3 million. [...] The congressman bought the complex in 2008, soon after securing the first of two earmarks for the two-mile project and unsuccessfully seeking millions more. The assessor's office now values the complex at $16 million, a 60 percent appreciation. (A1, A13)

"Restoring pride and self-respect to society's losers was a central platform in the social reforms that marked 20th century progress," Judt wrote: "Today we have once again turned our back on them" (27). In recent weeks, Issa has attacked what he calls "the culture of government overspending" and is "pushing for deep cuts in the national debt" (Lichtblau A13). It is bittersweet to remember the late 1970s when economists could assume that the percent of the people in poverty would continue to grow smaller on its own—that in a sense, we had conquered poverty in the United States.

But poverty is much worse than ever, and it's as though the national debt is being made the scapegoat for that and other problems much more serious than the debt. Judt argues that "the rising generation is acutely worried about the world it is to inherit" (3); is it that, or is it the national debt? The estimated Gross (accumulated) Federal Debt in 2010 was 13.8 trillion dollars (*Statistical Abstract* 2011, Table 468, page 310) and National Income in 2010, as estimated above, was 13.0 trillion dollars. The ratio of Gross Federal Debt to National Income was 1.06. This ratio is almost twice what it was in 2000 (Tables 467 and 672), when it equaled 5.6 trillion divided by 8.9 trillion, or approximately 0.63. However, the ratio 1.06 is not the highest it's ever been. In 1945, the Gross Federal Debt was 292.6 billion dollars (*Statistical Abstract of the United States:* 1950, Bureau of the Census, Table 383, page 339), National Income was 182.7 billion dollars (Table 315, page 264), and the ratio was 1.60. Three years later, in 1948, that ratio was down to 1.14, close to where it is now.

The most important attribute of the debt is not how big it is, but that it is payable in U.S. dollars, not foreign currencies or precious metals. The Federal Reserve Bank has the option, called Quantitative Easing, of buying back as much of the debt that it chooses with spendable dollars, which has the advantage in a recession or depression of stimulating demand for American goods and services. This being a major recession, it is beyond my understanding why Governor Rick Perry called such action "potentially 'treasonous,'" even warranting "'ugly' treatment should the chairman, Ben S. Bernanke, ever pay a visit to Texas" (Jeff Zeleny and Jackie Calmes, A14). I doubt that the governor meant this as a threat to the chairman's physical safety, but it does make me think of Faith trampling under foot the eyes of Worship-of-the-Old-Gods "and squeezing them out in death" (Thomson 281). That the governor connected Quantitative Easing to "[p]rinting more money" suggests why U.S. Treasuries are and will remain the safest possible dollar-denominated investment—deserving of a lowered credit rating only because of the as-yet-unheard-of-possibility that Congress *might* be able to willfully suspend interest payments due on them. True, the dollar itself is subject to inflation. My first acute sense of the value of a dollar came in January of 1946 when, upon entering college, my family had to pay $200 for my first semester's tuition. My father died near the end of the semester, and Harvard generously came through with a full-tuition scholarship beginning that fall. The cost of tuition at Harvard reached $35,000 a year in 2011, which seems like an inordinate rise, but represents the annual compounding, at 7.1216 percent interest, at which $400 grows to $35,000 in 65 years. Actually, this is more than the rate of inflation of consumer prices, which was 3.8243 percent from 1946 to 2010, the latest year included in the Web's *Inflation Calculator* (www.westegg.com/inflation/infl.cgi), and may reflect increasing relative costs of education and research over the last 65 years. The tuition example, however, illustrates how comfortably we have lived with inflation for a long time, which we can probably continue to do if our central government, which includes the Federal Reserve System, keeps it under control. An inflation rate between one and three percent is actually a good thing, especially during a recession, because it makes buying goods and investing in the present more desirable relative to postponement. The prospect of further *deflation* of the price of homes has been a persistent drag on the current housing market.

It was a surprise to read Paul Volker's Op-Ed piece, "A Little Inflation Can be a Dangerous Thing," in the September 19, 2011 issue of the *New York*

Times (A25). Volker, past chairman of the Federal Reserve from 1979 to 1987, thought we learned a lesson in the 1970s "when the word stagflation was invented to describe a truly ugly combination of rising inflation and stunted growth, [...] when "inflation becomes anticipated and ingrained" (A25). I remember those days when manufacturers were quick to raise prices. That ended in the 1980s when imports became competitive and a threat to domestic producers. I also remember, to my shame, when the trade deficits began seriously mounting, assuring my students, year after year, that the price of imports would soon be rising to equalize the playing field. I didn't realize until after I retired that China was quite comfortable tying its currency to the dollar and investing its trade surplus in dollar-denominated assets. Because of the globalization of production, I'm not sure that Volker is right that "we are on the edge today of serious inflation" though I agree with him that it "is unlikely if the Fed remains vigilant" (A25). If 2 percent inflation stimulates investment, I don't understand why, if it became "anticipated and ingrained," its "stimulating effects [would be] lost" (A25). I personally am suffering because government-insured instruments are paying only 1.35% at this time. If an inflation rate of say, 2 percent were anticipated, that interest rate would have been 2 percent higher. In his *General Theory of Employment, Interest and Money*, Keynes surmised that the abundance of capital in a stationary economy "ought to be able to bring down the marginal efficiency of capital in equilibrium approximately to zero" (220). In an article I published 25 years ago, I argued that the marginal efficiency of capital, which equals the interest rate when markets are in equilibrium, must be greater than zero in the real world in which the capital stock depreciates over time (Kohn *The Rate of Interest* 379n). I'm not sure what the implications of this result are for our present state in which the interest rate is hovering near zero.

Psychomachia or "The Fight for Mansoul"

Chapter Four

Musgrave's Generalization of Keynes's *General Theory*

The full-employment, stabilization theory that began with Keynes's *General Theory* "occupies but a third of the total space" in which Musgrave conceives "the revenue-expenditure process of government," traditionally referred to as public finance (vi, 3). What stands out in my memory from the many times I read *The General Theory* during my undergraduate years was Keynes's assertion that if people were unemployed and no work was available, they could usefully be set to digging holes in the ground for other unemployed workers to fill back up. The exciting consequence was that a dollar spent on unemployed labor would be spent by that worker on goods, the production of which would generate more wages, which when spent would generate still more, leading to an increase in wage income over time that far exceeded the initial dollar of public outlay. Musgrave gives an example of this multiplier process in which the total increments of generated income over time are five times the original outlay authorized by the idealized Stabilization Branch of the government (504). By including an Allocation Branch, Musgrave required that the original government outlays be spent on the projects with the highest ratios of total benefits to costs. Whereas Keynes focused on attaining full employment, Musgrave looked as well toward maximizing social welfare with the *optimal* combination of private and public goods and services. This was an important improvement, for as Benjamin Higgins wrote: "There is little in the *General Theory* on principles of planning public investment" (476).

I don't remember whether Keynes wrote about distributional equity, but I am unable to find that term or any terms relating to it in Seymour Harris's masterwork on Keynes. Musgrave, however, called for a Distribution Branch which could "conclude that distributional adjustments may be needed at times" (19), and perhaps, if income taxes must be raised to maintain the efficient level of public goods, make them more or less progressive, or in the absence of that option, alter the mix of public goods to benefit the economic class that needs relief. It may be that I am biased by my Worship-of-the-Old-Economics, but I believe we should be addressing our economic problems of Stabilization, Allocation and Distribution according to Musgrave's time-tested logic. To move the economy toward stability and full employment, we should focus on greater economic problems than the size of the federal debt, which might not even be a problem. I write this in full awareness that after Standard & Poor's downgraded their rating of long-term U.S. Treasuries, analysts did not expect this to shock financial markets because it simply confirmed, as Motoko Rich and Graham Bowley saw it, "what the markets, economists and most people already know: the United States has a debt problem and Washington is deeply divided over how to solve it" (1). In the section of his book on the burden of national debt, Musgrave addresses the social cost of interest and some technical issues, but says nothing about the ratio of total debt to current income (577-580). That ratio rises and falls with essential policy moves, and in the meantime the debt provides the safest dollar-based, government-guaranteed securities for investors. Indeed, Rich and Bowley went on to acknowledge that "the S.&P. downgrade left Treasuries near the top of a short list of assets attractive to investors anxious about Europe's debt crisis" (1).

The worse thing we can do, but which is now required by law, is to cut back on efficient government expenditures, knowingly increasing unemployment. This is what Krugman calls

> The Bleeding Cure [. ...] Fortunately, physicians no longer believe that bleeding the sick will make them healthy. Unfortunately, many of the makers of economic policy still do. And economic bloodletting isn't just inflicting vast pain; it's starting to undermine our long-run growth prospects. (A25)

This is the "Know-it-all" that the letter-writer in the *Post-Dispatch* on August 6, 2011 claimed lacked a "nuanced view of things," constantly whines "about opposing viewpoints," and cannot "engage in a dialogue on the merits of an issue without descending into childlike diatribes." I think that Krugman has come up with a brilliantly nuanced metaphor that makes dialogue almost superfluous. The "bleeding cure" is Keynesian economics in reverse. The Neo-Republicans counter that the Keynesian approach was tried by the second Bush Administration when, between December 2001 and December 2008, it increased the national debt 72 percent, from 5.8 to 10.0 trillion dollars, and still unemployment increased (*Statistical Abstract* 2011, Table 468). The potential efficacy of the Keynesian stimulus depends on the investment multiplier, which in the above example from Musgrave was assumed to be five. One of the reasons that the Keynesian approach has become less effective is that one of the "leakages" that reduce the multiplier is an excess of imports over exports. Deficit spending during World War II was especially efficacious because goods domestically consumed were almost necessarily produced in the United States. That war also required huge quantities of tanks, airplanes, battleships, etc., which also were produced domestically. In contrast, much of the heavy equipment used in the wars waged by the second Bush administration had already been produced in prior years, a greater proportion of war spending was outside the country, and, given the persistence of large annual excesses of imports over exports, the fiscal multiplier had to have been lower than it ever was. Finally, a large part of stabilization expenditures begun by the second Bush administration in 2008 were bailouts authorized by the Troubled Asset Relief Program (TARP) to prevent meltdowns rather than augment employment. It is not fair to say that Bush followed a Keynesian approach, which then failed.

    The Neo-Republicans reject Musgrave's Allocation Branch on principle. It has been their view that anything "the public sector could do private individuals could do better" (Judt 6). Even after April 20, 2010, when BP experienced the largest accidental oil spill in the history of the petroleum industry, and before the spill was capped three months later, the Obama Administration was widely criticized for not moving in immediately and stopping the contamination of the Gulf of Mexico. I don't believe that the federal government should be big enough to act on its own in every crisis, without the private sector, but it should be big enough to be respected for its competence. Yesterday evening (August 31, 2011), I was shocked to learn on the PBS NewsHour that tons of marijuana are being grown, illegally and surreptitiously in California's Mendocino State Park, most of it in cooperation with Mexican Drug cartels. I have nothing against marijuana, and have written articles advocating its being legalized and taxed (*New Close Readings* 188), but I was incensed at the videos of armed thugs defending their crops with automatic rifles in a public park. The perpetrators should know that they will ultimately face, not private security hirelings, not county sheriffs, not California riot squads, but the United States military and the highest federal administrative and judicial authorities. On the front page of the August 21, 2011 *New York Times*, William Broad announced that General Electric has finally perfected a process by which "enriched uranium—the fuel of nuclear reactors and bombs," can now be produced

> with nothing more substantial than lasers and their rays of concentrated light. [...] That might be good news for the nuclear industry. But critics fear that if [...] the secret gets out, rogue states and terrorists could make bomb fuel in much smaller plants that are difficult to detect. (1, 12)

What is most frightening is that the new process "can simplify the hardest part of building a bomb—obtaining the fuel" (12). One laser pioneer told Broad that: "If you could enrich with lasers, you could cut the cost by a factor of ten" (12). Advocates for the commercialization of the new technology argued "that the laser secrets had a low chance of leaking and that a clandestine plant stood a high chance of being detected" because "this was not something that would sit in a garage or be easily hidden" (12). Their critics, however respond that "a clandestine bomb maker would need only a tiny fraction of that vast industrial ability—and thus could build a much smaller laser, perhaps like the modest apparatus in the old photograph" that Broad described earlier in the article: an "old black-and-white photograph of the sensitive technology—perhaps the only image of its kind in existence publicly—shows an array of pipes and low cabinets about the size of a small truck" (12). "At least 20 countries," writes Broad, have investigated the laser technology, while "the overall number of scientists involved globally ran to several thousand" (12). Out of the blue,

> President Mahmoud Ahmadinejad in February 2010 praised Iranian scientists for their 'relentless efforts' to build lasers for uranium enrichment. Ever since, the I.A.E.A. has sought unsuccessfully to learn more. [...] Their concern goes to the nature of invention. The demonstration of a new technology often begets a burst of emulation because the advance opens a new window on what is possible. (Broad 12)

For a nation to survive in the hypermodern world ours has become, it needs a large, multi-faceted, efficient government. There are unforeseen synergies between the various branches, and we do not have the luxury of picking a few favored departments and leaving the rest to atrophy. The robustness of our human values as a nation requires national oversight from A to Z, from the Arts to Zooplankton, not just Defense and Intelligence.

Our most successful industries need oversight. The largest cell-phone operator in the U.S. wants to buy out a major competitor and control a larger fraction of the cellular market. We depend upon the economic and legal expertise of government servants empowered to resolve what could be a major threat to competition. Beside the deep-ocean drilling catastrophe discussed above, there has arisen the total surprise of shortages in cancer drugs. I say "total surprise," having chauffeured my wife through an intense six-months of chemotherapy for breast-cancer during the last six months of 2009. As recently as that, there was never a hint that these very expensive medicines would ever be in short supply. Many of us suddenly became aware, from a front page article in the August 20,

2011 issue of *The New York Times*, that federal officials and lawmakers, along with the drug industry and doctors' groups, were

> rushing to find remedies for critical shortages of drugs to treat a number of life-threatening illnesses, including bacterial infection and several forms of cancer. [...] So far this year, at least 180 drugs that are crucial for treating childhood leukemia, breast and colon cancer, infections and other diseases have been declared in short supply—a record number. (Gardiner Harris A1)

Harris detailed a number of reasons for the shortage, some validating the role of government regulation—as for example that "More than half the recent shortages have resulted because government or company inspectors found problems like microbial contamination that can be lethal upon injection"—some possibly unfavorable, at least from a libertarian point of view—such as a "disconnection between the free market and required government regulation" (A3). The strongest message that I take from Harris's article is that there have been immense advances in this country in medical technology—the shortages may be in part be problems caused by rapid growth. I credit Lyndon Johnson for this. When he established Medicare in the 1960s, most retired people went to doctors much less frequently than we do today. By subsidizing medical care for the aged, he increased the demand for it enormously, stimulating research and the development of remarkable new technologies. As quickly as we develop new approaches, we discover errors in the old. My wife, now a cancer-survivor, may have gotten the disease because, for years after menopause, she was on the widely-recommended estrogen and progesterone replacement pills, which were subsequently found to cause breast cancer and other illnesses. Because of the spectacular advancements in medical knowledge and technology and their stimulating, high multipler effects on related industries, investments in healthcare, both private and public, have contributed to islands of growing employment in a sea of unemployment. The New Health Care Law sparked by Obama may be one of the best stimulus programs of all. When the technological boom in chemotherapy begins to stabilize, patents on the extremely expensive infusions will run out and their prices presumably decline.

In their Op-Ed piece in the August 23, 2011 issue of *The New York Times*, Ezekiel Emanuel and Jeffrey Liebman suggest ways to cut Medicare costs that actually benefit patients. Improvements like these would unfetter funds that can be better used for younger people. Emanuel and Liebman usefully observe that

> when older adults are charged higher co-payments [for office visits and prescription medicines], they reduce their primary care visits and use of prescription drugs. But the research also shows that forgoing this outpatient care leads to an increase in expensive hospitalizations.

In my opinion as an 83-year old senior, older people are receiving scarce medical treatment that in many cases could be better used, at least provide benefits over longer expected lifetimes, by children and working adults. Based on the same general principle, we should perhaps consider imposing higher co-payments on medical bills as people age year-by-year. Beyond that, co-payments for elective procedures should be higher than for emergency procedures in the absence of which patients could not function, *e.g.*, be totally blind or bedridden. Such an effort to impose quasi-price constraints on demand, which are more socially acceptable if the distribution of income and wealth is equitable, should be augmented by committees staffed by doctors like Emanuel and Liebman, who are empowered to withhold costly procedures from elderly patients whose quality of life is marginal. I would much rather have committees of doctors like these two empowered at national and local levels cutting Medicare in ways they say help patients, than the six Democrat and Republican members of the special Congressional committee charged with recommending $1.5 trillion in deficit reductions over the decade, who Jackie Calmes and Robert Pear claim on today's front page of *The New York Times* have "expressed a willingness to wring savings from the long-untouchable [entitlement] programs" (A1). After "a shift of resources from the young to the elderly that dates back to the 1980s," a reallocation of medical resources from the old to the young is in order; Tavernise reports "an analysis of government transfers over time" by Robert Moffitt, an economist at Johns Hopkins University, which "found that aid to the elderly living on less than half of poverty-level income rose by 13 percent from 1984 to 2004, while aid to single-parent families in the same situation dropped by about 38 percent. The worst-off families have been left behind, Professor Moffitt said (*Poor Young* A19). While a shift in medical dollars from the old to the poor is called for, please oppose the Neo-Republican "Regulatory Time-Out Act" being considered in the Senate, which rolls back government regulations that protect the weaker among us, especially seniors, from health-threatening pollutants like ozone, mercury, sulfur dioxide, nitrogen oxides and coal ash. In this case, even Michael Mandel, chief economic strategist for the Progressive Policy Institute is going along with the Neo-Republicans: "While we're still in this downturn, I think it makes sense to delay or alter regulations in order to provide breathing room for the economy" (Bill Lambrecht A7). What about the breathing room in people's lungs?

In Musgrave's tripartite system, the authorization of equity enhancements is the responsibility of the Distribution Branch, which even more than the roles of the Allocation and Stabilization Branches, is disdained by Neo-Republicans. So great is inequality of income in the United States that we would surely be experiencing volatile extremes of social turmoil if it weren't for Social Security, Medicare and Medicaid. Most families have or have had members in one or more of these programs and appreciate that they are federally subsidized. Given the sad state of income and wealth distribution in the United States, it is all the more important that we improve such programs rather than wring savings from them in the name of the federal debt.

Early in 2007, in my final article as an economist, I concluded that "income inequality" in the United States "has increased to the point that, instead of expanding the economic pie, it is making it smaller" (*Inflated Executive Salaries* 116). I argued that inflated executive salaries, lobbying excesses, and exorbitant election campaigns were the consequence of greed encouraged by the pronounced decrease in the progressivism of income taxes, the large-scale removal of corporate dividends from the tax base, and the slashing of inheritance tax rates. It seemed to me that inflated executive salaries, lobbying excesses, and bloated election campaigns point to a greater dependence of the earnings of business executives on the favors of elected officials, especially since more and more lobbyists are carrying messages between them. Because election campaigns have become so costly, politicians need the financial support of corporations and their chiefs. The lowered tax rate on high incomes was a perfectly legal way for politicians to compensate for election contributions. The top court in the land, the Supreme Court, has elevated such contributions to a constitutional right, a new form of free speech. In a front-page article of the August 28, 2011 *New York Times*, Nicholas Confessore explained a 2010 Supreme Court Ruling that allowed independent political action committees, PACs,

> to raise and spend millions of dollars in unrestricted campaign donations—something presidential candidates are forbidden to do themselves [. ...] What took thousands of individual donations to make significant political advertisements in 2008 can now just take one phone call. (1, 4)

Buffett sounded a bit naive when he suggested that tax "blessings are showered upon [the mega-rich] by legislators in Washington who feel compelled to protect us, much as if we were spotted owls or some other endangered species. It's nice to have friends in high places" (A19). Many of the mega-rich pay generously for these blessings; if Buffett is not one of this *quid-pro-quo* elite, he should be commended for just free-loading. As for the new Super PACs, It's Christmas for consultants," Confessore reports, "It's completely unlimited. And it's going to change everything" (4). Instead of doing independent benefit/cost analyses for the federal government and promoting efficiency, consultants are advising electioneers. Instead of being based on principles of economic efficiency as Musgrave counseled, it may be more realistic to acknowledge that "fiscal policy, like other government policy" has become "fundamentally a political process," at least that's what Standard & Poor's David Beers says it is (Nelson D. Schwartz and Eric Dash 1). It has been a time-honored custom for most "wealthy members of Congress [to] push their financial activities to the side, with many even placing them in blind trusts to avoid appearances of conflicts of interest" (Lichtblau 1). That may be coming to an end as the highly visible congressman from San Diego demonstrates the profitability of "the hands-on-role he has played in overseeing a remarkable array of outside business interests since his election in 2000" (1). The favoritism that lobbyists can secure for their business clients, and some congressmen for themselves has been," called by Judt "a recipe for just those pathologies and inefficiencies normally associated with public ownership," which should, but apparently does not, shock those Americans who hate anything that smacks of Socialism (198-99).

Although it's been proved over and over again in welfare economics that when we properly measure the size of the pie in units of well-being rather than dollars an economic pie is bigger when resources are allocated efficiently rather than politically, my article on inflated executive salaries and the shrinking of the economic pie was roundly criticized because it wasn't backed up by evidence. Fortunately, since I wrote it, Richard Wilkinson and Kate Pickett have shown statistically that various indices of social dysfunction tend to be worse in countries where income inequality is higher. In his book, Judt reproduces their graphical results for such indices as social immobility (15), health and social problems (18), homicides (19) and mental illness (19). Most dishearteningly, the maximum rate of estate taxation, the least likely of all taxes to reduce work incentive—surely less than the *annual* tax that the rich pay on their total wealth in France and will again in Spain, which is moving to reinstitute its wealth tax—was slashed to 35 percent last November. Could that slash in the estate tax have been a pay-off to political donors? Even Sarah Palin has begun to realize that it's not *nothing* that "[political] donors expect from their investments" (Jeff Zeleny). It was in the middle of a talk in Iowa in which she advocated "the elimination of all federal corporate income taxes" that it dawned on her that "the cozy relationship between political contributions and government favors needed to be exposed and eliminated" (Zeleny). Why, Harwood asked, has Obama's message to raise taxes on the very wealthy and eliminate some of their unjustified loopholes "fared better with voters [...] than it has with Congress?" (A17). Why is it that "[p]olls show that most Americans side with President Obama on taxes for the wealthy," but that so "many in Congress do not" (A17). The very question supports my 2007 article on "Inflated Salaries, Lobbying Excesses, and Exorbitant Election Campaigns" and suggests that the votes that senators and representatives would gain by satisfying the general public's demand for greater fairness are less than the votes they would lose if they forfeited the donations that lobbyists marshalled from rich donors for their bloated election campaigns. These campaigns are fights for mansoul, and they play up to people's fears. "Polls show," writes Harwood, "that most Americans side with Mr. Obama on higher taxes for the wealthy. But voters are dispirited about economic conditions and with Mr. Obama's leadership in general, and he has been ineffective in pressuring Congress to go along" (A17).

Not only has democracy suffered, but so has the potential size of the economic pie. In his *New York Times* article on August 31, 2011, Kocieniewski reported that at "least 25 top United States companies paid more to their chief executives in 2010 than they paid to the federal government in taxes" (*Where Pay for Chiefs* B1). The companies averaged $1.9 billion each in profits, but "a variety of shelters, loopholes and tax reduction strategies allowed the companies to average more than $400 million each in tax benefits," while the "chief executives of those companies were paid an average of more than $16 million a year" (B1). A study by the liberal-leaning Institute for Policy Studies "suggested that current United

States policy was rewarding tax avoidance rather than innovation" (B5). It is innovation that makes the pie larger, not tax avoidance. This is the kind of empirical evidence that I needed in 2007 to argue that "income inequality has increased to the point that, instead of expanding the economic pie, it is making it smaller" (Kohn *Inflated Executive Salaries* 116).

*September 22, 2011: On this, the day I am to complete the book and send it to the publisher for formatting, there is finally some good news on the front page of the *New York Times* for my polemic. Keven Sack wrote that

> Young adults, long the group most likely to be uninsured, are gaining health coverage faster than expected since the 2010 health care law began allowing parents to cover them as dependents on family policies. [... I]n the first quarter of 2011 there were 900,000 fewer uninsured adults in the 19-to-25 age bracket than in 2010. (A1).

Psychomachia or "The Fight for Mansoul"

Chapter Five

Faith-Based Neo-Economics

I associated Faith, one of Prudentius's ardent Virtues in his fifth-century *Psychomachia*, with Neo-Republican politicians because of the latters' faith that steep cuts in the federal deficit achieved by curtailing government spending will spur employment and investment in America, even though economic logic provides no support for such causality. It turns out, to my surprise, that there are economists who encourage the Neo-Republicans. Binyamin Appelbaum has argued that "Economists agree that federal borrowing must be reduced, but they cannot agree about the proper mix of tax increases and spending cuts" (A11). He should have said that "*Some* economists agree that ..." for Krugman surely does not, but Appelbaum does refer to "One of the studies that found in favor of spending cuts" (A11). Although he did not identify that particular study, he quotes a line from it that I was able to Google and trace to a 2009 working paper, Number 15438, in the long-running series promulgated by the National Bureau of Economic Research. The paper is by Alberto Alesina and Silvia Ardagna, professors in the preeminent economics department of Harvard University. I have not looked at works like this since my retirement from economics in 1990, nor was I *ever* able to write such high-power statistical papers as theirs. It is replete with useful information, but I am dubious of its relevance to the controversy between raising income taxes versus lowering public sector expenditures in order to cut the federal debt. Though Alesina and Ardagna base their results on 198 episodes of fiscal stimuli and fiscal adjustments, only one of them took place in the United States (see their Table A1). That was a fiscal stimulus in 2002, under very different conditions than prevail today. Likewise, only 21 percent of the episodes in the other 20 countries took place after 1999, and only 4 as recently as 2007 (Table A1). The results of their model, in their words, "suggest that tax cuts are more expansionary than spending increases in the case of a fiscal stimulus"

53

(3). What we need to know in 2011 is whether a tax *increase* on the highest income earners in conjunction with fiscal spending increases can still be expansionary and, at the same time, reduce the national debt. Their model does not answer that question. Moreover, as noted earlier and is contrary to their results, the Bush tax cuts, ordained under the Economic Growth and Tax Reconciliation Act of 2001 and the Jobs and Growth Tax Relief Reconciliation Act of 2003, failed to achieve their objectives. The authors do, however, "uncover several episodes in which spending cuts adopted to reduce deficits have been associated with economic expansions rather than recessions," which supports their de-emphasis of fiscal spending increases and decreases. (Alesina and Ardagna 3). Unfortunately, we do not know whether these fiscal spending cuts occurred in *overheated* economies in which low priority government spending had been crowding out more efficient private investment. Their special case may also relate to that of Olivier Blanchard in which "a fiscal adjustment may be expansionary if agents believe that the fiscal tightening generates a change in regime that 'eliminates the need for larger, maybe more disruptive adjustments in the future" (4).

Whereas Alesina and Ardagna "find that "a 1% increase in the cyclically adjusted tax revenue decreases real growth by less than one-third of a percentage point" (5), it would surely be less than that under Obama's proposal to increase taxes only on incomes greater than $1,000,000, and then only back to the pre-Bush rates. At those high levels of income, a tax hike might come entirely out of planned savings so that spending would not be cut at all. Alesina and Ardagna do reinforce Obama's plea for aid to the unemployed when they note, "given the gravity of the crisis" that "an increase in the generosity of unemployed benefits seems quite warranted both in terms of social justice and in terms of sustaining aggregate demand, since the unemployed probably save very little anyway" (15). They also caution readers from the very beginning, that "we know relatively little about the effect of fiscal policy on [long-term] growth" (2). Nevertheless, "Republicans have embraced the study's conclusions without the caveats, extending the logic to argue that any revenue increase," even those derived by eliminating maladaptive loopholes in the tax system and obsolete subsidies, "would do more harm than good" (Appelbaum A11). Based on the NBER working paper, the House speaker, John A. Boehner, goes so far as to declare that a "tax hike would wreak havoc not only on our economy's ability to create private-sector jobs, but also on our ability to tackle the national debt" (A11).

If Boehner knows about Alesina and Ardagna's paper, which seems to be the case, so must the other major Neo-Republican players and/or their advisers. Economists are attracted to issues in the political spotlight. That was one of the reasons I wrote my doctoral dissertation on air pollution control and moved on to environmental economics. In 2001 I was attracted by the controversy over immigration to write a paper on "Immigration and Capital Transfers" that was pretty much "over the top." Having acknowledged the ongoing conflict between raising taxes and lowering government spending to counter deficits, Alesina and Ardagna may have felt challenged to argue for a solution that was counter-intuitive from the long-engrained Musgravian perspective. For them, the federal debt may be a disease, but it is not the worse economic problem they fear, which is inflation. They acknowledge that inflation

> has the effect of chipping away the real value of the debt but it may be a medicine worse than the disease. A period of controlled and moderate inflation would be a good debt deflating tool, but the risk of losing control of inflation is too big to try that strategy. It took a sharp recession in the early eighties to eliminate the great inflation of the seventies, and the last thing we need is another recession. (2)

Volker reiterated the fear of losing control of inflation, which I questioned earlier in this polemic. I agree with Alesina and Ardagna that a "controlled and moderate inflation" would be a "good debt deflating tool," but more importantly it is a feasible tool. The U.S. debt is denominated in dollars, not in a harder currency that is beyond our control. This is entirely different than the Greek debt, which is

Faith-Based Neo-Economics

owed in euros. There is no way that the Greeks can lend themselves euros to pay off their debts nor engineer moderate inflation on their own. I was shocked a week ago when I heard Douglas Holtz-Eakin, a former economics professor, former director of the Congressional Budget Office and now president of the American Action Forum, say of our country that "We are headed straight toward a Greek crisis"! This was in the segment entitled "Roundtable Part II, Plan for Jobs" on the September 4, 2011 edition of *This Week with Christiane Amanpour* on ABC. I remember when inflation went into the double digits and not liking it at all. Deep in the archives of the Carter administration there may still be the stupid letter that I sent the President complaining that the new Susan B. Anthony dollar, the size of a quarter, sent a terrible message for the value of our currency. There are much worse economic phenomena than immoderate inflation, among them; that one family has as much wealth as the bottom 120 million people in the country, that the laws now in place almost guarantee that this disparity will get worse and worse; that many of these 120 million adults and children have to get routine medical care, paid for by the government, in hospital emergency centers that are much more costly to operate than the family care practices which they can't afford; that this country had to go through the devastating collapse of the housing market which radiated adversely into multiple other markets; and that we can't adopt the kinds of regulations that will prevent reoccurrences because Neo-Republicans disdain the growth of government that new regulation entails. I would rather risk inflation in the teens than accept unemployment near the teens. I remember in the early 1980s when Murray Wiedenbaum, then Reagan's Chairman of the Council of Economic Advisors, told the country that double digit inflation was behind us. I was skeptical of his confidence, but he was absolutely right. Inflation proved easier to deal with than unemployment.

*Sunday, September 10, 2011: I have just learned that Tony Judt died on August 6, 2011 at the age of 62. I missed William Grimes's obituary, had not known that Judt had "Lou Gehrig's disease, which he learned he had in September 2008," that in "a matter of months the disease left him paralyzed and able to breathe only with mechanical assistance," and that he had "continued to lecture and write." "Last October," Grimes wrote that,

> wrapped in a blanket and sitting in a wheelchair with a breathing device attached to his nose, Mr. Judt spoke about social democracy before an audience of 700 at N.Y.U. He turned that lecture into a small book, *"Ill Fares the Land"*, published in March by Penguin Press.

I mention Judt's name more than twenty times in this polemic and had been looking forward to contacting him after it was published: Another sad disappointment.

**Wednesday, September 14, 2011: At least Tony Judt has been spared today's announcement that "Another 2.6 million people slipped into poverty in the United States last year, [...] and the number of Americans living below the official poverty line, 46.2 million people, was the highest number in the 52 years the Bureau [of the Census] has been publishing figures on it" (Tavernise *Poverty Reaches* A1).

***Wednesday, October 26, 2011: Today, the final day on which the last few corrections of my manuscript can be made, it was announced by Robert Pear in *The New York Times* that

> The top 1 percent of earners more than doubled their share of the nation's income over the last three decades, the Congressional Budget Office said Tuesday [. ...] "The equalizing effect of federal taxes was smaller" in 2007 than in 1979, as "the composition of federal revenues shifted away from progressive income taxes to less-progressive payroll taxes," [... F]rom 1979 to 2007, average inflation-adjusted after-tax income grew by 275 percent for the 1 percent of the population with the

highest income. For others in the top 20 percent of the population, average real after-tax household income grew by 65 percent. By contrast, the budget office said, for the poorest fifth of the population, average real after-tax household income rose 18 percent. And for the three-fifths of people in the middle of the income scale, the growth in such household income was just under 40 percent. (Pear)

This trend is unconscionable. The lowest fifth of the population get an 18 percent trickle-down, the middle class 40 percent, while the upper 1 percent, the country's vaunted engine of growth, keeps 275 percent more. Perhaps the housing bust that precipitated the crash in 2008 was in part a reflection of this shocking redistribution of after-tax income. It is ironical, in the face of evidence that the composition of federal revenue has shifted away from progressive income taxes to payroll taxes, that the "joint Congressional committee on deficit reduction is considering changes in a wide range of benefit programs" (Pear). It is too late for me to correct the *Works Cited* and *Index* for this final addendum, so I will note here the missing reference:

Pear, Robert. "It's Official: The Rich Get Richer." *New York Times* (October 26, 2011): A20.

Psychomachia or "The Fight for Mansoul"

Chapter Six

9/11 and the Re-recognition of Good Versus Evil

On September 8, 2011, I attended a panel discussion on how "9/11 Changed our Conversations," presented by Washington University's John C. Danforth Center on Religion and Politics. I was astonished at what I learned that night though, after thinking about it, more astonished that I had been astonished. The panelists, Marie Griffith, Bob Duffy and Andrew Rehfeld, made the point that 9/11 brought the conflict of Good and Evil back into contemporary conversation. I should have immediately remembered that; in my recently published book on Thomas Pynchon, I had written that his new novel,

> *Inherent Vice* proclaims Pynchon's implicit return to modernism's "absolute moralizing judgments," which postmodernism repudiated in the 1960s in favor of a "dialectic" which went "beyond good and evil," beyond the "sense of some easy taking of sides." (Kohn *New Close Readings* 163)

The phrases in quotation marks are from page 62 of Fredric Jameson's highly influential *Postmodernism or, The Cultural Logic of Late Capitalism*, which made clear when it was first published in 1991 that "good versus evil" had emblematized the utopian teleological modernism that postmodernism repudiated. Before 9/11, I thought that I had embraced the postmodern dialectic which went beyond good and evil, but when I saw Ana Juan's cover of the September 12, 2011 issue of *The New Yorker*, featuring the 2011 skyline of New York City with the reflection of the dream-like twin towers revivified in the water, it made me think of the two enormous sixth-century Buddhas of Bamiyan that the Taliban dynamited and demolished in March 2001. The latter was more grossly insensitive than evil, but the former was unmitigated Evil. Only recently have I begun to understand my shamefully uncontrolled anger in the two days following 9/11, when my wife and I were attending an Elderhostel at a Buddhist monastery; I subsequently regained some of my postmodern philosophy, though not to the extent that Don DeLillo abided by it throughout the 9/11 ordeal (see my *Tibetan Buddhism in Don DeLillo's Novels*, endnote 4).

My major interest in literary criticism was in defining postmodernism in a way that might explain why it came into existence and might help to identify its sequel. Because it was modern science and technology that underlay modernity's confident utopian expectations, it seemed to me that Paul Virilio's *fear* of hyper-science and hyper-technology—he called it "hypermodernism"—would be the sequel to postmodernism (Armitage; see also Kohn, *Pynchon Takes* 156, 178-9). When Condoleezza Rice said that September 11 taught us that we're vulnerable in ways that we didn't understand, in a new world in which the possibility of terrorism, married up with technology, could make us very, very sorry if we didn't act, and whoever heard of an airliner being flown into a building like a bomb, she echoed the fear of science and technology that Virilio was warning us against.

The second major point made by the panelists was that 9/11, united the country for a short period (Bob Duffy said that it "lasted until Halloween"), but then divided it as never before in recent times. Again, I should not have been surprised at that because I was already writing this polemic on Neo-Republican economics, which appears to have taken our country to a new level of polarity. Then I remembered the vociferous demands in this country for "Truth in 9/11." Truthers claimed that the World Trade Center buildings had self-destructed into their own footprints, exhibiting all the features of controlled demolition. Although dust samples collected included traces of nanothermite, an explosive compound which is mainly used by the U.S. military, I don't for a minute believe that U.S. agents planted explosives in the twin towers or the building next to them. However, there are multiple unexplained issues regarding the attack on the Pentagon that do make me suspicious.

Because Obama promised transparency and then, for whatever reason, did not provide information to counter the "Truthers," I became inclined to think that our government knew that bin Laden was hatching something here in America, most-likely having to do with flying a small two-engine airplane with explosives into the Pentagon, thought they had evidence that Iraq was behind the plot and considered it a moderately lethal provocation that would get us into a convenient war that could be easily and advantageously won. In the *New York Times*, Scott Shane wrote about "a former F.B.I. agent," Ali H. Soufan,

> who tracked Al Qaeda before and after the Sept. 11 attacks [… and] accuses C.I.A. officials of deliberately withholding crucial documents and photographs of Al Qaeda operatives from the F.B.I. before Sept. 11, 2001, despite three written requests, and then later lying about it to the 9/11 Commission. (A23).

Could it be that the public has been led to believe that the C.I.A. and the F.B.I. were too competitive over their respective turfs, in order to cover-up the real, unsavory truth behind 9/11? That the actual attacks were much more devastating than had been anticipated had to have been a great embarrassment, but the Administration made good use of it. Don DeLillo may have been as suspicious as I am, when he had his fictionalized version of the chief architect of the Iraq War declare:

> A great power has to act. We were struck hard. We need to retake the future. The force of will, the sheer visceral need. We can't let others shape our world, *our minds*. All they have are old dead despotic traditions. We have a living history and I thought I would be in the middle of it. (*Point Omega* 30)

To think that our own government invited a disaster, albeit much less catastrophic than it turned out to be, puts me along with others into the dystopian environment in which 9/11 has left us. With Good and Evil re-recognized, the postmodern era has ended. In my preceding book, I began to think that dystopia, which I associate with Franco Berardi, rather than hypermodernism (which I associate with Virilio), may be the more pervasive sequel of postmodernism (*New*

Close Readings 177, 180, 181), though both are founded on fear. Perhaps that fear is in part an outgrowth of the polarity to which 9/11 gave rise.

In the "Sunday Review" of the September 11, 2011 issue of the *New York Times*, I was saddened to discover the kind of Op-Ed piece that encourages the Neo-Republican economics that I fear—yes fear, these are dystopian times. It is by Robert Barro, already one of the leading American macroeconomists when I retired 21 years ago this month. He agrees

> that the recession warranted fiscal deficits in 2008-10, but the vast increase of public debt since 2007 and the uncertainty about the country's long-run fiscal path mean that we no longer have the luxury of combating the weak economy with more deficits. Today's priority has to be austerity, not stimulus, and it will not work to announce a new $450 billion jobs plan while promising vaguely to pay for it with fiscal restraint over the next 10 years, as Mr. Obama did in his address to Congress on Thursday. Given the low level of government credibility, fiscal discipline has to start now to be taken seriously. (Barro 8)

I wish that Barro had suggested something positive, like advocating legislation that would mandate reductions in the debt when prosperity returns and the federal government's revenue again exceeds its legitimate spending. Wouldn't such a law increase "government credibility" and send the right message for true fiscal discipline? How can Barro on the one hand agree that the recession warranted fiscal deficits in 2008-10, and then, on the other hand, speak of "the president's failed experiment" (8)? What kind of "[s]table expectations of a sound economic environment" can austerity and people losing their government jobs, even in the name of fiscal discipline, generate that Barro claims will "drive [private] investments?" (8). He has nothing to say about the growing inequality of income and wealth in the United States but advocates "the lowering of marginal income-tax rates for [all] individuals," the introduction of "a tax on consumer spending, like the value-added tax (or VAT) common in other rich countries," "abolishing federal corporate [income] taxes," "because of double taxation," and ending "estate taxes" (8). For Barro, the present "crises are opportune times for these important, basic reforms" (8). He writes that he "had a dream that Mr. Obama and Congress enacted [his] fiscal reform package—triggering a surge in the stock market and a boom in investment and G.D.P." (8). The dreamer is Faith personified. One of the world's most influential economists, Barro was acclaimed for his 1974 article "Are Government Bonds Net Wealth?" in which he concluded, for the case in which

> the marginal net-wealth effect of government bonds is close to zero, [...that] a change in the stock of government debt would have no effect on capital formation, and, more generally, [that] fiscal effects involving changes in the relative amounts of tax and debt finance for a given amount of public expenditure would have no effect on aggregate demand, interest rates, and capital formation. (1116)

Although I am unable to understand a lot of Barro's paper, his conclusion could support the neutrality of government debt in periods of excess unemployment.

*It is mid-October, 2011, and I am proof-reading the formatted pages of my polemic. Serendipitously, the October 10th issue of *The New Yorker* has an article on Keynes by the accomplished economics writer John Cassidy that allows me to check the current state of informed opinion on the mounting federal debt. He quotes Keynes's supportive view in 1931 that "budget deficits were a by-product of recessions, and that they served a useful purpose: 'For Government borrowing of one kind or another is nature's remedy, so to speak, for preventing business losses from being, in so severe a slump as the present one, so great as to bring production altogether to a standstill'" (Cassidy 48, 52). Despite such reassurance to the contrary, Cassidy suggests that "Keynes's knew what excessive government debts can do to an economy" and gives the presumably relevant example of the 1919 reparations that "saddled Germany and Austria with crushing debts" (54). Of course this "[o]utraged" Keynes; this was not a debt denominated in marks and owed mostly to Germans and Austrians, but an obligation to and in the currencies of the victor nations. In the case of *self-imposed* "deficits and debts," it was only when they "reached historically high levels," that Keynes had any reservations, and then, according to Cassidy, he simply found it "necessary [for policymakers] to spell out how they would be reduced in the long term" (54). This is exactly what I said on page 62 that Barro should have advocated in his September 11 Op-Ed piece. Keynes did believe that "large-scale deficit spending should be confined to recessions" (54), a rule which the second Bush Administration so glaringly and unfortunately violated, both by reducing the Musgravian tax rate **t** and increasing the corresponding rate of government spending **g**. According to Cassidy, Barro now believes that the multiplier for public deficit expenditures

> is close to zero: for [... w]henever individuals see the government boosting spending [...] on a temporary basis, [...] they figure that these policies will eventually have to be paid for in the form of higher taxes. As a result, they set aside extra money in savings, which cancels out the stimulus. (Cassidy 52)

For Barro to offer as likely, an extreme case in which the multiplier is close to zero, is irresponsible.

Psychomachia or "The Fight for Mansoul"

Chapter Seven

Dystopia and Neo-Postmodernism

I began this polemic with the hope of understanding Neo-Republican economics from the perspective of Prudentius's moral Virtues, fighting the good fight for God. I was able to see how the Neo-Republican politicians might identify their Virtues with Righteousness, Soberness, Thrift, Faith and Long-Suffering and perceive their enemies, the Vices, as Worship-of-the-Old-Gods [of Economics], Indulgence, Lust, and Deceit. For my approach I depended on an intertextual reading of the early fifth-century *Psychomachia*, sections of my old Musgrave text, Tony Judt's final book, and, to bring it all into the present, *The New York Times* from August 5, 2011, when I began the polemic, until September 22 when I completed it for formatting. A relic myself of the old modernist utopianism, I quickly learned from these newspaper articles that the times are "out of joint," that "something is rotten in the State of Demark," and that the debt crisis, to which Democrats as well as Republicans defer, is at worst a scapegoat for deeper problems. My gut fears got away with me when I read Ryan Lizza's article on Michelle Bachmann. A contender for the Republican nomination to oppose President Obama in 2012, Bachmann told Lizza that she admired Francis Schaeffer, "a major contributor to the school of thought now known as Dominionism, which relies on Genesis 1:26, where man is given dominion "over every creeping thing that creepeth upon the earth" (Lizza 58). Bachmann called him a "tremendous philosopher," who "wrote marvelous books and was very inspirational" (59). In 1981, three years before his death, Shaeffer published *A Christian Manifesto,* his "guide for Christian activism, in which he argues for the violent overthrow of the government if Roe v. Wade isn't reversed" (Lizza 59). Surely I am wrong to think that any Neo-Republican politician would have an open mind for an American revolution to overthrow the government. But then, I fail to understand why so many Republicans insist on the right of Americans to own AK-47 assault rifles. Why are they so intent on weakening the Federal Government? Why do they ignore impassioned calls for sacrifice on the part of the wealthy to match that of the middle class and poor? It is almost a provocation that they refuse to consider eliminating tax loopholes and specially-discounted income tax rates for hedge fund managers. Could they actually be inviting angry protests in the streets, gun violence, and an excuse for crackdowns by a self-appointed emergency government? If that is the case, this country is indeed devolving into an uglier dystopia. This includes myself for harboring thoughts that the second Bush administration may have intentionally left the country vulnerable to an attack by Al Qaeda. In a front-page article in the September 3, 2011 *New York Times*, Michael Shear quoted Governor Perry as writing that the "federal income tax was the 'great mile-stone on the road to serfdom,'" that Social Security is "a crumbling monument to the failure of the New Deal" that it is a Ponzi scheme" and "a monstrous lie on this [younger] generation" (A1, A11). Such sea-changes in government policy that Perry calls for could be realized in America only by fascistic fiat, mandated by a self-proclaimed non-democratic emergency government. And wouldn't they be proud to order a patriotic balanced budget amendment for the Constitution?

It brought Prudentius to my mind when Berardi wrote in his new book published earlier this month, that for "the people of the Middle Ages, living in the sphere of a theological culture, perfection was placed in the past, in the time when God created the universe and humankind" (*After the Future* 18). *Pschomachia* was written in 405, twenty-seven years after Emperor Valens was defeated by the Visigoths at Adrianople and five years before the Visigoths under Alaric sacked Rome. From 400 to 402, "the Goths who were settled in the Balkans and Illyria made a move towards Italy [, in] late 401, they besieged Milan, where the emperor Honorius was, and unleashed a wind of fear that reached Rome" (Lançon 36). Honorius must have been "His Grace the Emperor," who, as Prudentius wrote in 405, "advanced me in his service and raised me up," and who would likely have seen to it that Prudentius was apprised of the difficulties that the Roman Empire was experiencing with the Visigoths (Thomson 3). Presumably, Prudentius was still living in May 408 and would have learned of Alaric's demand for "a sum of 4000 gold *librae*, equal to 288,000 *solidi*" not to attack Rome (Lançon 37). I am grateful to Luisa Bagiotti for advising me by email that the "golden solidus was introduced by Constantine," that "it weighed 4.548 grams" so that "Alaric asked for 1.31 tons of gold." That translates into approximately $76.5 million at the current price of $1825 per ounce of gold. In its day, 4000 gold *librae* were "the equivalent of the annual property revenue of a senatorial family" (Lançon 37). Rome "had restored its defense wall in 402-3," and although it "had no adequate garrison," its 800,000 (Lançon 14) residents "had taken up arms and been trained to handle them" (37). Alaric had hoped "to obtain a treaty of alliance from Honorius, together with lands and positions of command [typically such lands served us a buffer, and the Goths their defenders, against the threatening Hun invaders from the north], as well as the 4,000 gold *librae*, but the Emperor, ensconced in near impregnable Ravenna, refused,

> and the siege of the city began in December[, 408. ...] Famine, then epidemics, began to sap the Romans' physical strength and morale. They had to make do with half, then a quarter, of their usual daily bread ration. [...] A Roman embassy handed over 5000 gold and 3000 silver *librae* to the Goths, together with 4000 silk garments, 3000 scarlet hides and 3000 *librae* of pepper, entirely provided by the senators. [...] Alaric allowed the Romans to come to Portus [, the harbor at the mouth of the Tiber river,] for three days to get fresh supplies. [...] Taking advantage of greater freedom of movement, slaves fled and joined the besiegers. (Lançon 37)

By the summer of 410, "in a state of utter physical and psychological exhaustion," the Roman defenders stood aside as the Goths entered the city and

> "indulged in pillage for three whole days [...] There were fires, murders and kidnappings for ransom purposes. Some Romans were able to seek

shelter in St. Peter's basilica, which the Goths [being Arianist Christians] respected. On 27 August, they left Rome for the south, with considerable booty and distinguished hostages" (Lançon 38).

We see in The Fall of Rome, what Berardi may be seeing in the present: "historical existence tak[ing] the shape of The Fall, the abandonment and forgetting of original perfection and unity" (*After the Future* 18).

What the Romans experienced was worse than our 9/11—"As the dead could no longer be buried outside the *pomerium*, 'the city became the tomb of the dead,' writes Zosimus" (Lançon 37)—and yet Prudentius remained utopian, for in his *Psychomachia*, good invariably triumphs over evil; in dystopia, the opposite is expected. Prudentius optimistically saw Rome's problem as its outmoded pagan religion and its worship of the old gods. "Although the expression 'end of the Roman Empire' can make sense," concludes Lançon,

> the fall of Rome' has no historical reality. Rome did not fall, but was transformed [. „,] In the fourth century, many writers had the feeling that Rome was enjoying a venerable old age, but educated Christians spread the idea that Christianity might give it renewed youth. By doing so they were resuming the theme of renewal and regeneration that was recurrent in the empire's history. Shortly after 400, Prudentius was a witness to this transition and upholder of this *renovatio*" (Lançon 163).

This witnessing on Prudentius's part was most triumphant when he rhetorically asked in *Psychomachia* whether bold Judith, slayer of Holofernes, "prefigured our times, in which the real power has passed into earthly bodies to sever the great head by the hands of feeble agents? Well, since a virgin immaculate has borne a child, hast thou any claim remaining [...] ?" (Thomson 285). Prudentius thus contrasted the faith in God-became-man with what he perceived to be the lower orders of Christian faith of the fourth-century teacher Arius, "which deny the divinity of Christ" and simply "define the relation of Christ to God according to natural reason" (Edwin Knox Mitchell 281). It was "Christianity in its Arian form" that had been accepted by the Goths and "reached the other early Germanic invaders before they entered the empire" (John McNeill, 655). Though "the sack of Rome in 410 had enormous repercussions throughout the empire" (Lançon 39), Prudentius's utopian pride was sustained by the Catholic Christology.

In contrast, Berardi carries on at length about the dystopia of the "vertiginous zero zero decade" (*After the Future* 11). During the "last three decades of the [20th] century," as he sees it, "the *utopian imagination* was slowly overturned, and has been replaced by the *dystopian imagination*" (17). Berardi provides pages and pages of historical facts to prove his pessimistic claim. Alternatively, I argue in "Pynchon Takes the Fork in the Road" and *New Close Readings of* "The Crying of Lot 49" that utopian modernity ended during the 1960s, that it was postmodernism that prevailed the rest of the century, and that hypermodernism or/and dystopia began in the 2000s, though my interpretation is based mainly on novels of Pynchon and DeLillo, both of whom appear to have been early readers of Virilio and Berardi. Neither of the latter recognize postmodernism; Berardi wrote that utopia gave "birth to the kingdom of dystopia" (26) while Virilio told Armitage that modernism just became worse and worse until it was hypermodernism. Both Virilio and Berardi exaggerate the disabling effects of hyper-science and hyper-technology on the human mind, but do not cite medical sources to back-up their pessimistic claims. Nevertheless, their fears for human sanity could explain what is different about dystopia in our time as opposed to Prudentius's. What other than science and technology is so different today that Berardi is impelled to warn "the young readers" of his book "to pay attention: a gigantic wave of desperation could soon turn into a suicidal epidemic that will turn the first connective generation into a devastating psychic bomb" (*After the Future* 39). The closest that I can come to consciously experiencing dystopia is to watch Van McElwee's video *Liquid Crystal,* which can be readily found and downloaded on the internet, an experience that I describe in an article entitled

Dystopia and Neo-Postmodernism

"The Motorization of Video Art." Warning: my wife won't watch this video and gets upset if she even hears the sound track from another room. Another good friend, who is a professional artist, walked out of the theatre minutes after the beginning of its premier showing in St. Louis. I can only hope that the present polemic, which I am self-publishing, will be half as effective as *Liquid Crystal* is in projecting dystopia.

Based on my abstract model of cultural-aesthetic periods, in which utopian modernity was repudiated and followed by American postmodernism in the 1960s, the first novel to be called postmodern was probably Pynchon's *The Crying of Lot 49*. Because the ethos of postmodernism inspired a wide-ranging variety of enticing stylistics, the term stayed current until almost the end of the century (see McHale and my *Pynchon's Transition*). Then modernism surfaced again, at first I thought as hypermodernism, in which the prior utopianism was replaced by fear. Subsequently, while writing my *New Close Readings,* I began to think that it had resurfaced as dystopian modernism. If it was the former, DeLillo picked up on it in his novel *White Noise* (161). If it was the latter, DeLillo was already on to it in *Mao II*, as was William Gaddis in *Carpenter's Gothic*. In *Inherent Vice*, Pynchon traced dystopia back to the Los Angeles of 1969. It occurs to me that hypermodern can be considered as a special case of the more general dystopian modernism, so that it is not a case of one *or* the other.

James Rives called my attention to Thomson's translation of *"non simplex natura hominis"* (Line 904) as "man's two-sided nature," to which he preferred "the un-simple nature of man." I now realize that five lines later, Prudentius wrote *"distantesque animat duplex substantia vires"* (Line 909), which Thomson translated as "and our two-fold being inspires powers at variance with each other" (342, 343). I had not looked at that second line in the Latin before and therefore had not called it to James's attention, but it does seem to have justified Thomson's preference for "man's two-sided nature." This self-revelation on Prudentius's part resonates in the closing lines of *Psychomachia*:

Psychomachia or "The Fight for Mansoul"

> Savage war rages hotly, rages within our bones, and man's two-sided nature is in an uproar of rebellion; for the flesh that was formed of clay bears down upon the spirit, but again the spirit that issued from the pure breath of God is hot within the dark prison-house of the heart, and even in its close bondage rejects the body's filth. Light and darkness with their opposing spirits are at war, and our two-fold being inspires powers at variance with each other, until Christ our God comes to our aid, orders all the jewels of the virtues in a pure setting, and where sin formerly reigned builds the golden courts of his temple, creating for the soul, out of the trial of its conduct, ornaments for rich Wisdom to find delight in as she reigns for ever on her beauteous throne. (Thomson 343)

We now understand why in the grand preface to all of his poems, Prudentius refers to his soul as though that part of him is feminine. This essence of himself combines Vices as well as Virtues, all of whom are women. Though they are at variance with each other, Good invariably triumphs over Evil. This was utopianism thirteen or fourteen centuries before its classic modern counterpart. It could represent Neo-Republicanism, seeing herself as "mighty Wisdom [, who] sits enthroned and from her high court sets in order all the government of her realm, mediating in her heart laws to safeguard mankind" (341), except that the Neo-Republican version of Prudentius never hints at foul desire, at the dark prison-house of the heart, or his/her own body's filth. Only if it did could Neo-Republican Economics rise above dystopia. In my *New Close Readings*, I perceive a new postmodernism which repudiates the otherness of evil in the new dystopian modernism, just like the old postmodernism repudiated the abiding goodness in the old utopian modernism. Gerald Early saw it first when he told an audience attending a panel discussion on John Adams' *Death of Klinghoffer* at the Ethical Society of St. Louis on May 26, 2011 that to rise above evil, to even recognize it,

> you must first know how seductive evil can be, how it can give false strength and corrupted pride. [...] To believe that evil is found only in the

> other, that evil is the other, is merely to delude ourselves by believing that what is horrible in human beings is alien to us. Nothing humans do is alien to any other human being. (*New Close Readings* 182)

When she generously read my polemic manuscript for errors, Luisa Bagiotti noted a fascinating parallel between the final sentence of the above excerpt and 2nd century B.C. Roman playwright Terence's "I am a man: nothing human (no human thing) is alien to me" ("*Homo Sum: humani nihil a me alienum*") from the comedy *Heautontimoroumenos*.

Only when the Neo-Republicans can see faults of the Worshippers-of-the-Old-Gods in themselves, and we Worshippers-of-the-Old-Gods can see the faults of the Neo-Republicans in ourselves can there be the civility of Neo-Postmodernism. I fear that neither the Neo-Republicans nor I can get past the anger that besets us. In this polemic I have only been able, through *Psychomachia*, to make moral sense of Neo-Republican Economics from their own perspective, not my own. Although I am one of the disaffected base that Zeleny and Thee-Benan described on the front page of the September 17, 2011 *New York Times*, I have to credit President Obama for rising about hatred, though I wonder if he too has been hampered by utopianism. What I can say for myself (sadly, because I am not a politician) is that I have at last gotten past my outmoded utopianism. I was horrified to read about the dystopia at the Human Development Corporation of Metropolitan St. Louis in the recent *Post-Dispatch* article by David Hunn:

> The nonprofit had mismanaged state contracts to serve families in poverty, overcommitted federal dollars to contractors and overspent to the point where it couldn't even meet payroll, the Missouri Department of Social Services alleged. Furthermore, the nonprofit had collected $4.2 million in federal grants to pay utility costs for thousands of low-income St. Louisans this year, yet hadn't paid at least $650,000 that it collected. (A13)

To its credit, the Human Development agency's board finds the situation "very alarming" and acknowledges that, although the "agency does retain certain non-liquid assets, [...] its cash situation is extremely dire, with virtually no cash on hand and liabilities exceeding $1 million" (A13).

The following week, in an article by Steve Giegerich, *St. Louis Post-Dispatch* readers learned of new fallout from the cancellation of a State contract with the Indianapolis-based company SynCare, whose responsibility was

> to assess the Medicaid eligibility of more than 50,000 homebound patients for medical and personal services. The deal was terminated three months [after it started in May] amid myriad complaints and a failure to deliver the contracted services. [...] Along with the failure to complete assessments, the company came under heated criticism for the operation of a call center where telephones went unanswered for hours on end (A1, A11).

Much of my confidence in Musgrave's Allocation Branch in based on his textbook's focus on efficient quantities of public goods and services, especially those which poor people merit, and its affirmation of the capability of the public sector to administer or oversee their efficient distribution. The examples of the Human Development Corporation and SynCare help me understand why Neo-Republicans disdain big government, though it seems that where federal funds are being distributed through private or non-profit organizations, the government should have on-site accountants, paid by Washington, to track what is going on and blow whistles whenever they are called for. But I'm less confident than I used to be that even this would suffice. Actually, the SynCare debacle first hit the front page with its emphasis on political shenanigans. One of the Missouri officials who evaluated the $5.5 million state Medicaid contract and "signed off on the hiring of SynCare [...] ended up on the company's payroll" six months later, violating the Missouri conflict-of-interest statute that no state employee "use his decision-making authority for the purpose of obtaining a financial gain" (Steve Giegerich and Jim Doyle A1, A4). On its 2010 financial statement, Clayton, Missouri "based Centene Corp.—one of the state's biggest political donors and a leading Medicaid contractor nationally [...] calls SynCare a 'variable interest entity' of Centene and notes that the Company (Centene) is the primary beneficiary" (A1, A4). Giegerich and Doyle go on to explain that companies "use 'variable interest entities' for a variety of reasons but often as a kind of Trojan-horse strategy to operate with a low profile in a new market, exploring its potential without risking a substantial investment" (A4). Centene donates heavily to politicians and parties, including Gov. Jay Nixon" (A4). Moreover, the

> company's lobbyists in Jefferson City include attorney Chuck Hatfield, a longtime Nixon political adviser. [...] Since January 2006, Centene and its executives have given more than $400,000 in campaign contributions to dozens of Missouri politicians, including about $85,000 to Democrat Nixon; about $25,750 to Democratic Attorney General Chris Koster; about $19,500 to Republican Auditor Tom Schweich; and about $12,625 to Republican Lt. Gov. Peter Kinder. (A4)

Although state records show that SynCare bid considerably less for the contract than its competitors, "SynCare did not provide enough staff to handle the job it agreed to perform" (A4). Just as the vice chairman of the Human Development Board of Metropolitan St. Louis acknowledged that "anytime you hire a relative [the janitor?] and you don't have a good reason for it, it looks bad" (Hunn A13), so also does it look bad when a corporation like Centene donates $85,000 to the gubernatorial candidate of a state whose prospects, as its chairman and chief executive acknowledged: "We're evaluating" (Giegerich and Doyle A4).

Whereas Prudentius hoped for the day when "Christ our God comes to our aid, orders all the jewels of the virtues in a pure setting, and where sin formerly reigned builds the golden courts of his temple" (Thomson 343), I hope for the day when Musgravian progressive income taxes reign again, the problem of income inequality diminishes, and there is no longer the dystopia of inflated executive salaries, lobbying excesses, and exorbitant election campaigns. Given the enormous income of a Roman senator, equivalent to approximately 76.5 million of our dollars *per year*, and the fact that the Great Constantine, "by the promotion of heads of families of equestrian rank from Rome and the western provinces," had increased their number to 2,000 during his reign, I wonder whether, at its peak, the Roman Empire had its own problems of income inequality (Lançon 48).

Picking up on my concern as to whether the inequality of income and wealth had been a problem for the Roman Empire, Luisa Bagiotti advised me in an email dated September 23, 2011 that "the idea that Rome was declining starts appearing in authors of the golden age, as a consequence of civilian wars and widespread corruption," She helpfully provided a link to the Preface of *The History Of Rome* by Titus Livius, who lived from 59 B.C. to 17 A.D. and is known in English as Livy. His Preface concluded with an appeal that

> every man apply his mind seriously to consider [… how] their empire was acquired and extended; [but] then, as discipline gradually declined, […] sunk more and more, then began to fall headlong, until […] the present times, when we can neither endure our vices, nor their remedies. [… T]here never was any state either greater, or more moral, or richer in good examples, nor one into which luxury and avarice made their entrance so late, and where poverty and frugality were so much and so long honored, so that the less wealth there was, the less desire was there. Of late, riches have introduced avarice, and [a longing for] excessive pleasures […], amidst luxury and a passion for ruining ourselves and destroying every thing else.

The moral peak of the Roman Empire that Livy referred to, when poverty and frugality were honored, would have been, based on Luisa's email, "its apex in the II century B.C." How different the values that Livy enunciated from the "obsession with wealth creation" in the "contemporary United States, [where] at a time of growing unemployment, a jobless man or woman is thus stigmatized" (Judt 2, 24). Despite the reality of growing avarice, three and a half centuries passed before Prudentius wrote *Psychomachia*, and Rome was sacked five years later. If Livy's Preface reflects the values that endured in Rome, this might explain why the Empire lasted as long as it did. Not long ago, such values prevailed in America, but ended, and what

> has most drastically changed in the twenty-first century are the decreased progressivism of income taxes, the large-scale removal of corporate dividends from the tax base, the curtailment of inheritance taxes, […] and as a consequence of the scaled-up monetary windfalls, a greater reliance on lobbyists and the enriching *quid pro quo* that they can deliver. (Kohn *Inflated Executive Salaries* 115).

In effect, the tax changes at the beginning of the millennium have increased the riches of the of the wealthy and fomented a polarizing avarice that is ruining ourselves and destroying our country.

Psychomachia or "The Fight for Mansoul"

Chapter Eight
Conclusion

Berardi's 2009 book, *The Soul at Work*, was completed just after the economic crash of 2008. I had saved the front page of the *St. Louis Post-Dispatch* from September 26, 2008 because of its extraordinary headline which read:

NO DEAL • AS BAILOUT PLAN CRUMBLES, BUSH ISSUES WARNING:
'This sucker could go down'

Berardi wrote that the "dark side of the soul—fear, anxiety, panic and depression—has finally surfaced after looming for a decade in the shadow of the much touted victory and the promised eternity of capitalism" (*The Soul* 207):

> The final collapse of the global economy [...] is now unfolding under the eyes of an astonished mankind. Economists and politicians are worried: they call it a crisis, and they hope that it will evolve like the many previous crises that disrupted the economy in the past century but finally went away, leaving Capitalism stronger. I think that this time is different. This is not a crisis, but the final collapse of a system that has lasted five hundred years. (*The Soul* 210)

Berardi blamed the "amphetamine therapy [that] was prescribed by George W. Bush in the form of war and tax reductions for the wealthy. Bush issued an invitation to go shopping and actually facilitated an unprecedented increase in private and public debt" (209-10). By the time he wrote his 2011 book, Berardi was sure that the cause of the 2008 five-hundred-year crash was in the short run the "huge debt accumulated for the rescue of the banks" (141) and in the long run, a "the financial debt that the West (especially the US) has taken on during recent decades" (*After the Future* 157). There you have it: both the far right and the

Conclusion

far left and many of the people in between including our President, blaming our economic problems on the national debt. Everyone tells everyone else that the sky is falling, everyone believes it must be falling, but no one knows why.

Taking my cue from Musgrave, I have endeavored in this polemic to calm the fear over the public debt. The ratio of the total debt to national income has been higher before than it is today. I did not think to compare the ratio of our annual deficit to our national income with that of other countries and was pleased to happen upon Raphael Minder's article on Spain's plan to reinstate a wealth tax, that included this useful piece of supporting information: the Spanish "government has pledged to lower the budget deficit to 6 percent of gross domestic product this year, from 9.2 percent last year" (A3). Perhaps, I feared our comparable ratio would be as high as 20 percent or more. With census data for the United States that I used early in Chapter Three, I was able to calculate that the U.S. ratio of the estimated Gross Federal Deficit in 2010 to National Income was 1.4/13.0, which equals 10.8 percent. To compare the U.S. ratio with that of Spain, I needed, rather than the National Income, our Gross National Product for 2010, which was an estimated 14.6 trillion dollars—obtained by dividing "Receipts" for 2010 from the first column of Table 467, *Statistical Abstract of the United States 2011*, by the corresponding fraction, 0.148, in the seventh column— which yielded a deficit ratio of 1.4/14.6, or 9.6 percent. This is less than a half percent above Spain's ratio. True, Spain is one of the worrisome countries in Europe; however, Spanish banks cannot create Euro credits for their government whereas the Federal Reserve Bank can create dollar credits for ours.

Nor had I thought to compare total national debt with total household wealth or whether such a ratio would even be available. Fortuitously, the September 17, 2011 issue of the *New York Times'* Business Section had an article entitled "Household Net Worth Falls 0.3% in Quarter" which reveals that

> Household net worth dropped 0.3 percent to $58.5 trillion in the April-June quarter from the prevailing period, according to the Federal

Reserve's Flow of Funds report. The decline followed three straight quarterly increases. (B3)

Strangely, at least for me, the names of the authors had been omitted. Fortunately, an article entitled "Stock, House Values Cited in Decline of Wealth in U.S." appeared in the business section of that same day's *Post-Dispatch* with the missing names: Christopher S. Rugaber and Dave Carpenter, Associated Press. The content is not identical—for example, in the case of the above *Times* excerpt which includes "April-June quarter from the prevailing period, according to the Federal Reserve's Flow of Funds report." the *Post's* read "April-to-June quarter, according to the Federal Reserve's Flow of Funds Report released Friday." The next sentence was identical in both papers. Presumably, the individual newspapers edit the Associated Press articles to their liking. I shall assume in my Works Cited that Rugaber and Carpenter are the authors of the *Times* article.

Given the estimate of Gross National Debt of $13.8 trillion at the end of 2010 from Table 468 of the Statistical Abstract of the United States, and the Household Net Worth three months later, it follows that the U.S. Government's total debt is approximately one-fourth of its households' net worth. That does not seem like an alarming percentage to me, especially since we are ignoring the value of property and land owned by the Federal Government, which surely is in the trillions and trillions of dollars. But even then, I don't think of the federal debt only as a burden. It is also a symbol of investments made by the federal government over the years—the defeat of Hitler, National Parks, the Golden Gate Bridge, the St. Louis Arch, Interstate Highways, medical care for the poor and aged, mass transit, and a federal program that I first learned about yesterday morning when I serendipitously met Tony Glover, Assistant Director of the St. Louis Board of Education's "A+ Schools Program," the goal of which, in his words, is to ensure that St. Louis's high school students "are well prepared to pursue advanced education and employment." Their federal grant provides money for disadvantaged college-bound students to fulfill that dream. This includes

Conclusion

systems that people like Glover are developing to keep their aspiring charges on track. This program, like the others, is a wonderful investment in America's future, surely one for "rich Wisdom to find delight in as she reigns for ever on her beauteous throne" (Thomson 343).

The national debt of the United States is not the pressing problem that, according to President Obama, 80 percent of Americans think it is. As a percent of current national income, it is considerably less than the highest it's been in the last 60 years. It is only a fourth as much as the net wealth privately owned by Americans. Although it is growing with public expenditures to stimulate employment of idle resources, the annual budget deficit is less than 10 percent of annual gross national product. The debt is represented by Treasury securities owned for the most part by Americans and treated as wealth. The interest and principal are paid in U.S. dollars, whose relative stability is managed by the government on behalf of the people. The investment projects that the debt made possible were authorized by democratic processes and continue to provide public benefits that exceed their original costs. Blown out of all proportion as a problem, the national debt has unfortunately become the tail wagging the dog. It's even worse than that, as if they've straight-jacketed the dog to pare down its paws as well as its tail.

Psychomachia or "The Fight for Mansoul"

Epilogue

I completed the manuscript for this book near the end of September, left it with the publisher for formatting and, with all but the task of indexing remaining, departed St. Louis for a ten-day cruise of the Greek Islands and surroundings. The cruise, planned by my wife months before I ever thought of writing this book, culminated in a single afternoon that was nothing less than transformative. That was the afternoon that Martha and I disembarked at Kusadasi, a seaport on the west coast of Turkey, hired a taxi and drove fifteen kilometers to what had been, in the golden age of Rome two millennia earlier, the Empire's second largest city, Ephesus. Home to a population of "more than 200,000" it was the stunning capital of Rome's Asian province and the pride of visiting emperors, Augustus, Tiberius, Domitian and Hadrian (Selahattim Erdemgil 7). Because it was not excavated until the 1980s and 90s, I had never heard of Ephesus and expected to find no more than a few broken pillars and chunks of marble inscribed with Latin letters. Although 85 percent of the area remains to be excavated, partial renovations of once-stately buildings, some two-stories tall, are in startling evidence, their marble arches resplendent in sunlight again. What had been the central public latrine looked palatial. We walked the mile-long restored street, much of it the original marble pavement. Polished stone blocks, some inscribed in Greek, some in Latin, appeared to jumble third century B.C. relics of the earlier Greek city--that flourished in the wake of the victory of Alexander the Great over the preceding Persian masters--with those of the Romans that later merged with the Greeks. On closer inspection, the Latin and Greek inscriptions appeared to have been carved at the same time, suggesting that the Romans venerated their magnificently articulate Greek forebears and sought to keep their language alive. That would explain why Prudentius gave his famous poem its Greek title, *Psychomachia*. Our cruise ship offered sea-to-land email, and I was able to confirm this supposition with Luisa Bagiotti, who informed me by return mail that

Epilogue

The cultivated Romans, since the middle of the II century B.C., certainly knew Greek very well, and would go to Athens to learn philosophy, or to Rhodes or Asia Minor to learn rhetorics. [...] Greek names for Latin books are common even before the II century, which is the one during which the two cultures most productively mingled. Virgil's books, for example, have Greek titles: Bucolicon/ Georgicon/ Aeneidos.

In that same spirit, thanks to Luisa's scholarship, I herewith copy the original Greek rendition of *Psychomachia* that she emailed to me: ΨYXOMAXIA, which are the Greek letters Psi, Upsilon, Chi, Omicron, Mu, Alpha, Chi, Iota and Alpha. It speaks to the importance of their Grecian heritage that Ψ was the only one of these letters that the Romans did not borrow for their own alphabet.

Interspersed among statues of pagan gods, we found stones inscribed with Christian crosses, confirming the presence of both religions in Ephesus. When I asked Luisa if she believed that the apostle Paul lived in Ephesus as Erdemgil claimed (11), she emailed her assent because St. Paul had "travelled so much" and his "letter to the Ephesians" was well-known. Indeed, I remembered glancing at "The Epistle of Paul the Apostle to the Ephesians" in my copy of the *Christian Bible*, but never gave a thought to whom the Ephesians were. According to sources quoted by Luisa, Paul lived in Ephesus "for almost 3 years," performing "numerous miracles, healing people" and organizing "missionary activity into the hinterlands," but had to leave because of "a pro-Artemis riot involving most of the city." Only fifty years after Christ, the fight between Pagans and Christians for "mansoul" was in full swing in the Roman Empire. For me, the crown jewel of extant Ephesus was the two-storied, marble-pillared, statue-graced Celsus Library, "built on the tomb of Roman senator T. Iulius Celsus Polemaenus" during "the first quarter of the 2nd century" (Erdemgil 30). This library, already 270 years old when Prudentius wrote the preface for his poems, boasted 12,000 scrolls. It attests to its lasting importance that the Celsus Library was one of those featured in a distinguished series of Thursday-evening lectures on "Antiche Biblioteche" that Luisa Bagiotti and her mother had attended in the spring of 2011 in Milan.

It engrossed me that Erdemgil construed the sculpture of a beautiful woman in the portico of the Celsus Library as "representing the character of Celsus," for that supported my gender-based interpretation of Prudentius's soul "singing of her Lord" (Thomson 5). Whereas I had treated Prudentius's poetry largely as a foil for my own political economic ends, the aura of Ephesus happily reabsorbed it into "the glory that was Greece and the grandeur that was Rome" (Edgar Allan Poe, *To Helen*). Some part of me longed for a deeper connection to this place, which I recognized later when one of the people from our ship who had taken the group tour through Ephesus told me that they were shown the carving of a menorah along the walk. There must have been Jews living here, which I subsequently confirmed from my *Christian Bible* in which Saint Paul "came to Ephesus, [...] entered into the synagogue [...] and reasoned with the Jews" (*Acts* **18**:19). Could I have been related to any of those Jews? That was a hundred generations ago, and, assuming that there were no intermarriages between any of my antecedents in the same generation, there would have been 2^{100} of my direct ancestors (great-great- .... -great grandparents) living in 50 A.D. That is an enormous number--greater than the number of humans *combined* that will ever have lived on this planet--so there had to have been a huge number of intermarriages across my direct ancestors through the past two millennia. This would have been especially true for a people, such as mine, who were so often segregated from non-Jews. Surely some, if not most of the Jews with whom Paul reasoned, especially the Kohenim among them, are my direct forbears, and part of my heritage is Ephesian. Taking that 2 to the 100th power metaphor even further, St. Paul and Jesus himself would at the least have been my distant cousins.

I had bad experiences on our vacation as well as good. The original flight from New York to Athens and its replacement were consecutively cancelled; we missed the first three nights of the cruise, and stewed in the same dirty clothes for

Epilogue

four days. Still, I cherish the night spent at a seaside hotel in Kusadasi--waiting for our missed ship to harbor there the next morning for its scheduled visit to Ephesus--because it made me mindful that back in the golden age of Ephesus, which was the seaport back then, Kusadasi was part of the ocean floor--that much has plate tectonics, more specifically earthquakes, transformed the geography of that part of the world (see Essay Five of my *New Close Readings*). Ephesus is now kilometers from the sea. It was unfortunate that we missed the first two days of our cruise and had to fly to Istanbul, rather than to Athens, then on to Izmir and by bus to Kusadasi, but I have a better geographical feeling for Ephesus than I would have had if we had come by sea. In her email to the ship on October 5, 2011, Luisa Bagiotti put our situation in historical context by informing us that "uncertainty was a mark of all journeys in ancient times, so you can take them as an emotional surplus to your diving into antiquity."

I have quoted Luisa many times in this book, and should explain how she fits into my life. Her mother, Anna Bagiotti Craveri, is the past editor of *Rivista Internazionale di Scienze Economiche e Commerciali (RISEC)* and was well-known to many of the world's economists. By accepting and publishing six of the papers that I submitted to her during the 1980s and 1990s, she did more than most people to encourage my professional development. I took it as an honor that two of these papers became the lead articles in their respective issues. Martha and I had visited her 20 and then 15 years ago in Milan, and this vacation provided the opportunity for us to see her a third time. Despite her age, she took a two-and-a-half-hour train ride from Milan early in the morning to meet our incoming ship in Venice, spent some wonderful hours with us, then took the long train ride home, all in one day. Not only had she been important to me in economics, but she followed my career in literary criticism with determination, reading my essay in the journal *Religion & Literature* on *The Crying of Lot 49* by Thomas Pynchon, then the novel itself in the original English and finally, to be sure that she hadn't overlooked anything, reading the Italian translation of the novel as well. She is the kind of reader I had in mind when I wrote my first literary book, *New Close Readings in "The Crying of Lot 49,"* and I am grateful to her for offering to read it. Actually, Anna has an advanced degree in English, but had to enter economics after her husband died in 1983 to take over his duties as managing editor of the journal he had co-founded.

When, during the course of writing this paper I was unable to calculate the dollar equivalent of the 4,000 gold *librae* that the Visigoth Alaric demanded of the Roman Emperor, it was the natural thing for me to ask Anna for help. What I didn't know was that her daughter Luisa teaches history, Latin and other courses in the humanities at the Liceo Scientifico Statale Leonardo da Vinci in Milan, so that Anna was able to forward my emailed query to her personal expert in the field. Luisa seemed so happy to help me that I dared to broach the suggestion that she read the entire manuscript, which by then was almost complete. Of course, it was as easy and as fast to send it electronically to her in Italy as it later was to send the finished manuscript to my nearby publisher. Luisa generously set aside two days to read the manuscript, corrected many of the errors, one of them truly monstrous, and provided related information, much of which I have incorporated in the above chapters. She also opened my mind to new possibilities and sent me to original sources that I could never have accessed on my own. It was also Luisa's idea that I reformat the final lines of *Psychomachia* as free verse so as to tease out its poetic rhythm. When she subsequently wrote me that my "reformatting of Thomson's translation sounds very good," I knew that I had found my Muse.

Works Cited

Appelbaum, Binyamin. "Politicians Can't Agree on Debt? Well, Neither can Economists." *New York Times* (July 18, 2011): A11.

_____ and Catherine Rampell. "From Big Spending to Big Cuts, All While the Economy Stalls." *New York Times* (August 1, 2011): A1.

Armitage, John. "From Modernism to Hypermodernism and Beyond: An Interview with Paul Virilio." *Theory, Culture and Society* 16.5/6 (1999): 1-23.

Barro, Robert J. "Are Government Bonds Net Worth." *Journal of Political Economy* 82.6 (Nov. - Dec., 1974): 1095-1117.

_____. "How to Really Save the Economy." *New York Times: Sunday Review* (September 11, 2011): A1.

Berardi, Franco "Bifo." *The Soul at Work: From Alienation to Autonomy.* Translated by Francesca Cadel and Guiseppina Mecchia. Los Angeles: Semiotext(e), 2009.

_____. *After the Future.* Translated by Arlana Bove, Melinda Cooper, Erik Empson, Enrico, Guiseppina Mecchia, and Tiziana Terranova. Edinburgh: AK Press, 2011.

Bowley, Graham. "Stocks in Worst Tumble in 2 Years Amid Global Worry: Fear of Recession and Debt Crisis Drive Selloff." *New York Times* (August 5, 2011): A1, B6.

Broad, William J. "Laser Advances Raise Fears of Terrorist Nuclear Ability." *New York Times* (August 21, 2011): 1, 12.

Buffet, Warren E. Stop Coddling the Super-Rich." "*New York Times* (August 15, 2011): A19.

Calmes, Jackie, and Robert Pear. "A Bipartison Move to Cutting Benefits Programs." *New York Times* (September 9, 2011): A1, A14.

Carroll, Joseph. *Literary Darwinism: Evolution, Human Nature, and Literature.* New York: Routledge, 2004.

Cassidy, John. "The Demand Doctor: What would John Maynard Keynes tell us to do now—and should we listen?" *The New Yorker* (October 10, 2011): 46, 48, 52, 54, 56, 57.

Confessore, Nicholas. "Lines Blur Between Candidates and PACs with Unlimited Cash." *New York Times* (August 28, 2011): 1, 4.

DeLillo, Don. *White Noise*. New York: Penguin, 1986.

_____. *Mao II*. New York: Viking, 1991.

_____. *Point Omega: A Novel*. New York: Scribner, 2010.

Emanuel, Ezekiel J., and Jeffrey B. Liebman. "Cut Medicare, Help Patients." *New York Times* (August 23, 2011): A21.

Erdemgil, Selahattin. *Ephesus*. Istanbul: Net Turistik Yayinlar, 2011.

Gaddis, William. *Carpenter's Gothic*. New York: Viking, 1985.

Gershon, Michael D. *The Second Brain: The Scientific Basis of Gut Instinct and a Groundbreaking New Understanding of Nervous Disorders of the Stomach and Intestine*. New York: HarperCollins, 1998.

Giegerich, Steve. "State Tackles SynCare Backlog." *St. Louis Post-Dispatch* (September 16, 2011): A1, A11.

Harris, Seymour E. *The New Economics: Keynes' Influence on Theory and Public Policy*. New York: Knopf, 1948.

Harwood, John. "Campaign Redux as Obama Pushes for Taxes on Rich." *New York Times* (September 19, 2011): A17.

Hernandez, Raymond. "G.O.P. Legislators Balk at a Call to Tie Storm Aid to Budget Cuts." *New York Times* (September 7, 2011): A24, A25.

Higgins, Benjamin. "Keynesian Economics and Public Investment Policy." Seymour E. Harris, Ed., *The New Economics: Keynes' Influence on Theory and Public Policy*. New York: Knopf, 1948, 468-481.

Horwitz, Paul. "How to Respond to 'The Response'." *New York Times* (August 6, 2011): A17.

Hunn, David. "Janitor's Role Adds to Woes of Nonprofit: Chief of Agency Accused of Misusing Funds Paid Live-in Boyfriend $ 10,000 a Month." *St. Louis Post-Dispatch* (September 10, 2011): A1, A13.

Jameson, Fredric. *Postmodernism: Or, The Cultural Logic of Late Capitalism*. Durham: Duke UP, 1991.

Judt, Tony. *Ill Fares the Land*. New York: Penguin, 2010.

Knowlton, Brian. "Republican Lawmakers Equate Obama Tax Plan with 'Class Warfare.'" *New York Times* (September 19, 2011): A25.

Kohn, Robert E. "Leaf Burning: An Economic Case Study," *Scientist and Citizen*, April, 1967, pp. 71-75 (reprinted in S. Novick and D. Cottrell, editors, *Our World in Peril: An Environmental Review*, Greenwich: Fawcett Publications, 1971, pp. 419-426).

_____. "The Rate of Interest in a Stationary Economy." *Journal of Macroeconomics* 8.3 (Summer 1986): 373-380.

_____. "Thresholds and Complementarities in an Economic Model of Preserving and Conserving Biodiversity," *Socio-Economic Planning Sciences* 33 (1999): 151-172.

_____. "A Hechscher-Ohlin-Samuelson Model of Immigration and Capital Transfers." *Open Economies Review* 12.4 (October 2001): 379-387.

_____. "Postmodernist Manichaean Allegory in William Gaddis's *Carpenter's Gothic. Style* 40.4 (Winter 2006): 334-345.

_____. "Inflated Executive Salaries, Lobbying Excesses, and Exorbitant Election Campaigns." *Atlantic Economic Journal* 35 (2007): 115-116.

_____. "Pynchon's Transition from Ethos-based Postmodernism to Late-Postmodern Stylistics." *Style* 43.2 (Summer 2009): 194-214.

_____. "Unwitting Witness for Postmodernism." *Journal of Modern Jewish Studies* 8.3 (November 2009): 309-335.

_____. "Pynchon Takes the Fork in the Road." *Connotations* 18.1-3 (2008/2009): 151-182.

_____. "The Motorization of Video Art: Van McElwee's *Liquid Crystal* through the Lenses of Virilio and Berardi." *Afterimage: The Journal of Media Arts and Cultural Criticism* 37.6 (May/June 2010): 13-16.

_____. "A Derridean Look at the Paintings of Bessie Lowenhaupt." *Soundings* XCIII, 3-4 (Fall/Winter 2010): 385-407.

_____. *Close Readings of* The Crying of Lot 49, St. Louis: MiraDigital, 2011.

_____. "Tibetan Buddhism in Don DeLillo's Novels: The Street, The Word and The Soul." *College Literature* 38.4 (Fall 2011): 156-180.

Kocieniewski, David. "Where Pay for Chiefs Outstrips U.S. Taxes." *New York Times* (August 31, 2011): B1, B5.

_____. "A Tax Others Embrace, U.S. Opposes." *New York Times* (September 21, 2011): B1, B2.

Krugman, Paul. "The Bleeding Cure." *New York Times* (September 19, 2011): A19.

Lambrecht, Bill. "GOP Takes on Regulations." *St. Louis Post-Dispatch* (September 15, 2011): A1, A7.

Lançon, Bertrand. *Rome in Late Antiquity: Everyday Life and Urban Change, Ad 312-609*. Trans., Antonia Nevill. Edinburgh: Edinburgh UP, 2000.

Lichtblau, Eric. "Helping His District and Himself." *New York Times* (August 15, 2011): A1, A13.

Livy (Titus Livius). *The History of Rome: Translated by D. Spillan*. London: Henry G. Bohn, 1853.

Lizza, Ryan. "Leap of Faith: The Making of a Republican Front-Runner." *The New Yorker* (August 15 & 22, 2011): 54-63.

McHale, Brian. *Postmodernist Fiction*. London: Routledge, 1996.

McNeill, John T. "Christianity." *Encyclopedia Americana: International Edition, Volume 6*. Danbury: Grolier, 1993, 647-663.

Minder, Raphael. "Spain to Reinstate Wealth Tax It Dropped 3 Years Ago." *New York Times* (September 16, 2011): A3.

Mitchell, Edwin Knox (Revised by Martin R.P. McGuire). "Arianism." *Encyclopedia Americana: International Edition, Volume 2.* Danbury: Grolier, 1993, 281.

Musgrave, Richard A. *The Theory of Public Finance: A Study in Public Economy.* New York: McGraw-Hill, 1959.

Nocera, Joe. "How Democrats Hurt Jobs." *New York Times* (August 23, 2011): A21.

Pappe, Ilan. *The Ethnic Cleansing of Palestine.* London, Oneworld Publications, 2007.

Pynchon, Thomas. *The Crying of Lot 49.* Philadelphia: Lippincott, 1966.

_____. *Inherent Vice.* New York: Penguin, 2009.

Rich, Motoko, and Graham Bowley. "Markets Expected Credit Ruling, But Risks Remain, Analysts Say." *New York Times* (August 7, 2011): 1, 14.

Rives, James B. "Christian Expansion and Christian Ideology." *In W.V. Harris, Ed., The Spread of Christianity in the First Four Centuries: Essays in Explanation.* Leiden: Brill, 2005, 15-41.

Rugaber, Christopher S., and David Carpenter, "Household Net Worth Falls 0.3% in Quarter." *New York Times* (September 17, 2011): B3.

Sack, Kevin. "More Young Adults Insured Since Health Law Took Effect." *New York Times* (September 22, 2011): A1, A3.

Shane, Scott. "9/11 May Have Been Stopped but for High-Level Dysfunction, Ex-F.B.I. Agent Writes." *New York Times* (September 12, 2011): A23.

Shear, Michael. "Perry's Blunt Views in Books Get New Scrutiny as He Joins Race." *New York Times* (September 3, 2011): A1, A11.

Steinhauer, Jennifer. "Republicans, Fresh from Debt Battle, Set Sights on Balanced Budget Amendment." *New York Times* (August 5, 2011): A10, A14.

_____. "Fight Harder, Voters Telling Congressmen." *New York Times* (August 12, 2011): A1, A13.

_____. "For Some in G.O.P., a Tax Cut Not Worth Embracing." *New York Times* (August 26, 2011): A18.

Tavernise, Sabrina. "Poverty Reaches a 52-Year Peak, Government Says." *New York Times* (September 14, 2011): A1, A19.

_____. "Poor Young Families Soared in '10, Data Show." *New York Times* (September 20, 2011): A19.

Thomson, H.J. *Prudentius, Volume I.* Cambridge, MA: Loeb Classical Library, 1949.

Volker, Paul A. "A Little Inflation Can be a Dangerous Thing." *New York Times* (September 19, 2011): A25.

Westen, Drew. "What Happened to Obama?" *New York Times* (August 7, 2011): 1, 6-7.

Wilkinson, Richard, and Kate Pickett. *The Spirit Level: Why More Equal Societies Almost Always Do Better.* London: Allen Lane, 2009.

Zeleny, Jeff. "In Iowa, Palin Hints at Faults in Field." *New York Times* (September 4, 2011): 18.

_____. and Megan Thee-Brenan. "In Poll, Support for Obama Slips Among Base." *New York Times* (September 17, 2011): A1, A3.

Index

A+ Schools Program, 79
Ahmadinejad, Mahmoud, 45
Alaric, 66, 67, 85
Alesina, Alberto, 53-55
Alexander the Great, 81
Allocation Branch, 24, 26, 41-43, 48, 73
Al Qaeda, 61, 66
Amanpour, Christiane, 56
American Action Forum, 56
American Family Association, 8
Apocrypha, 16
Appelbaum, Binyamin, 5, 53, 55
Ardagna, Silvia, 53-55
Arius, Arian, Arianist, 68
Armitage, John, 60, 69

Bachmann, Michelle, 65
Bagiotti, Luisa, 6, 67, 72, 75, 81-85
Balanced Budget Amendment, 5, 66
Barro, Robert, 62, 63, 64
Benefit/Cost Analysis, 27, 28, 49
Berardi, Franco, 61, 77
Bernanke, Ben S., 39
Blanchard, Olivier, 54
Bleeding Cure, 42, 43
Blind Trusts, 50
Boehner, John A., 55
Boeing Corporation, 31
Bowley, Graham, 5, 42
BP Spill, 43
Broad, William, 44, 45
Budget Control Act of 2011, 29
Buffett, Warren, 34, 49
Bush, George W., 6, 12, 33, 43, 54, 64, 66, 77

Calmes, Jackie, 39, 47
Cantor, Eric, 10, 17, 31
Carpenter, Dave, 79

Carroll, Joseph, 8
Cassidy, John, 63, 64
Carter, Jimmy, 56
Celsus Library, 82, 83
Centene Corporation, 73, 74
Christ, Jesus, 4, 6, 12, 15, 68, 71, 74, 82
Christian, Christianity, 6-8, 11-13, 15-17, 19, 21, 56, 65, 68, 81, 82
Christology, 69
C.I.A., 61
Clinton, Bill, 33, 36, 37
Confessore, Nicholas, 49
Constantine, 67, 75
Craveri, Anna Bagiotti, 84
Crying of Lot 49, 84

Danforth Center for Religion and Politics, 59
Dash, Eric, 50
Debt, National or Federal, 15, 24, 27, 38, 42, 43, 48, 53-56, 62, 63, 77-79
Debt Battle, Ceiling, Crisis, Problem, 5, 13, 23, 42, 65
DeLillo, Don, 60, 61, 69, 70
Derrida, Jacques, 13
Distribution Branch, 26, 41, 42, 48
Distributional Equity, 15, 23, 25, 41, 47
Dominionism, 65
Double Taxation, 15, 23, 33, 34, 63
Doyle, Jim, 73, 74
Duffy, Bob, 59, 60
Dystopia, Dystopian, 10, 25, 28, 61, 62, 65, 66, 68-72, 74

Early, Gerald, 71
Earmarks, 28, 37
Economic Growth and Tax

92

Reconciliation Act of 2001, 54
Eisenhower, Dwight, 36
Emanuel, Ezekiel, 47
Environmental Protection Agency, 27
Ephesus, Ephesians, 81, 82, 83, 84
Erdemgil, Selahattim, 81, 82, 83
Executive Salaries, 49, 50, 52, 74

F.B.I., 61
Federal Reserve Bank, Federal Reserve System, 38, 39, 40, 78, 79
Fine-Tuning, 26, 27

Gaddis, William, 70
Galileo, 11
General Electric, 44
Gershon, Michael, 20, 21
Giegerich, Steve, 73, 74
Glover, Tony, 79
Goldsmith, Oliver, 35
Graves, Tom, 20
Griffith, Marie, 59
Grimes, William, 56, 57

Harris, Gardiner, 46
Harris, Seymour, 41
Harvard University, 39, 53
Harwood, John, 35, 51
Hatfield, Chuck, 74
Health and Social Problems, 50
Health-Threatening Pollutants, 48
Hernandez, Raymond, 10, 17
Higgins, Benjamin, 41
Holofernes, 16, 68
Holtz-Eakin, Douglas, 56
Homosexuality, 8, 9
Honorius, 66, 67
Horizontal Equity, 33, 34
Horwitz, Paul, 6-8, 15
Human Development Corporation of Metropolitan St. Louis, 72

Hunn, David, 72, 74
Hypermodernism, 60, 61, 69, 70

"Ill Fares the Land", 35, 37
Immigration, 55
Imports, Exports, 40, 43
Income Inequality, 35, 48, 50, 52, 63, 74, 75
Interdisciplinarity, 10
Intertextuality, 10, 65
Inflation, 24, 39, 40, 55, 56
Innovation, 52
Institute for Policy Studies, 51
Iraq War, 61
Issa, Darrell, 37, 38

Jameson, Fredric, 8, 59
Jewish, Judaism, 6, 7, 14, 16, 25, 71, 83
Jobs and Growth Tax Reconciliation Act of 2003, 54
Johns Hopkins University, 48
Johnson, Lyndon B., 46
Juan, Ana, 59
Judith, 16, 68
Judt, Tony, 26, 35-38, 43, 50, 56, 57, 65, 76

Keynes, John Maynard, Keynesian, 40, 41, 43
Kinder, Peter, 74
Klinghoffer, Death of, John Adams, 71
Knowlton, Brian, 6, 29
Kocieniewski, David, 33, 51
Koster, Chris, 74
Krugman, Paul, 9, 13, 23, 42, 43, 53
Kusadasi, Turkey, 81, 84

Lambrecht, Bill, 48
Lançon, Bertrand, 16, 66-69, 75
Leaf Burning, 27
Leakage, 43
Libertarian, 46

Index

Liceo Scientifico Statale Leonardo da Vinci, 85
Lichtblau, Eric, 37, 38, 50
Liebman, Jeffrey, 47
Liquid Crystal, 69
Livy (Titus Livius), 75
Lizza, Ryan, 65
Lobbying Excesses, 49, 51, 74, 76

Maffitt, Robert, 48
Mandel, Michael, 48
Mansoul, 12, 51, 82
Marginal Cost, 27, 28, 30
Marginal Revenue, Marginal Revenue Product, 30
McElwee, Van, 69
McHale, Bryan, 11, 70
McNeil, John, 69
Medicaid, 48, 73
Medicare 46-48
Middle Class, 5, 34, 66
Mill, John Stuart, 29
Minder, Raphael, 78
Minimum Wage, 33
Missouri Department of Special Services, 72
Mitchell, Edwin Knox, 68
Modernism, Modernity, 25, 59, 60, 69-71
Multiplier, 41, 43
Musgrave, Richard A., 23-27, 29, 33, 34, 36, 41-43, 48, 50, 64, 65, 73, 78
Muslim, 7

National Bureau of Economic Research (N.B.E.R.), 55
National Labor Relations Board, N.L.R.B., 31
New Health Care Law 2010, 46, 52
Nixon, Jay, 74
Nixon, Richard, 26
Nocera, Joe, 30, 31

Obama, Barack, 6, 15, 20, 31, 43, 46, 51, 54, 60, 62, 63, 65, 72, 80

Palin, Sarah, 51
Pappe, Ilan, 7
Paul the Apostle, 82, 83
Payroll Tax, 30, 34
Pear, Robert, 47
Perfect Allocation, 27, 28
Perry, Rick, 6-8, 15, 28, 38, 66
Personal Indebtedness, 35
Personal Responsibility and Work Opportunity Act, 36, 37
Pickett, Kate, 50
Pines, David, 9
Plate Tectonics, 84
Poe, Edgar Allen, 83
Political Action Committees (PACs), 49
Postmodern, Postmodernism, 59, 60, 61, 69-72
Poverty, Poverty-Line, Poverty-Level, 17, 30, 34, 36, 38, 57, 72
Progressive Policy Institute, 48
Prudentius, *passim*
Public Finance, 23, 24, 26, 41
Psychomachia, "The Fight for Mansoul," 4, 6, 7, 11-13, 19, 23, 51, 53, 65, 68, 70, 72, 76, 81, 82, 85
Pynchon, Thomas R, 84

Quantitative Easing, 38, 39

Rampell, Catherine, 5
Ratio of Annual Deficit to Gross National Product, 78, 80
Ratio of Annual Deficit to National Income, 78
Ratio of Total National Debt to National Income, 38, 42, 80

Ratio of Total National Debt to
    Private National Net Worth, 78,
    80
Reagan, Ronald, 26, 28, 56
Regulatory Time-Out Act, 48
Rehfeld, Andrew, 59
Rice, Condoleeza, 60
Rich, Motoko, 42
Rives, James, 10, 13, 17, 19, 20
*Rivista Internazionale di Scienze
    Economiche e Commerciali (RISEC)*,
    84
Rugaber, Christopher S., 79
Ryan, Paul D., 29

Sack, Kevin, 52
Samuelson, Paul, 9, 28
Schaeffer, Francis, 65
Schwartz, Nelson D., 50
Schweich, Tom, 74
Second Brain, 19, 20
Shane, Scott, 61
Shear, Michael, 66
Single-Parent Families, 48
Slaves, 67
Socialism, 23, 28, 50
Social Justice, 54
Social Problems, 35, 50
Social Security, 30, 48, 66
Soufan, Ali H., 61
Southern Poverty Law Center, 8
Stabilization Branch, 25-27, 30, 41,
    42, 48
Stagflation, 40
Standard & Poor, 5, 42, 50
Steinhauer, Jennifer, 5, 20, 30, 31
Stomach, *Stomacho*, 13, 14, 19-21
Stylistics, 70
Supreme Court, 49
Syncare, 73, 74

Tavernise, Sabrina, 34, 48, 57
Tax Loopholes, 6, 29, 51, 55, 66

Terrence, 72
Thessalonica, Edict of, 6
Thomson, H.J., 4, 6, 11-14, 16, 17,
    19, 20, 39, 67, 68, 70, 71, 74, 80,
    83
Transfer Payments, 36
Troubled Asset Relief Program
    (TARP), 43
Truthers, 60

Unemployment, Unemployment
    Benefits, 54, 76
Utopia, Utopian, 10, 25, 28, 36, 59,
    60, 65, 68-72

Value Added Tax (VAT), 63
Vertical Equity, 29, 34
Vestal Virgins, 17
Virilio, Paul, 60, 61, 69
Volker, Paul, 39, 40, 55

Wal-Mart, 35
Washington University, 19, 59
Westen, Drew, 34, 35
Wiedenbaum, Murray, 26-28, 56
Wilkinson, Richard, 50
Worship-of-the-Old-Gods,
    Worship-of-the-Old
    Economics, 15, 16, 23, 39, 42,
    65

Zeleny, Jeff, 39, 51, 72

www.ingramcontent.com/pod-product-compliance
Lightning Source LLC
Chambersburg PA
CBHW051736170526
45167CB00002B/964